To Kristi
Happy Cooking.

NEVER COOK BACON NAKED

...and other excellent advice, tips, secrets, and killer recipes from
Chef Dallas of the Tenth Street Basque Café

Chef Dallas

NEVER COOK BACON NAKED

Additional copies of this book can be ordered online as a hardcopy or as an "E"
Book at:
Nevercookbaconnaked.com

Through the official restaurant website at:
Tenthstreetbasquecafe.com

Via snail mail:
Tenth Street Basque Café
249 10th Street
P.O. Box 128
San Miguel, California 93451

Or by phone:
(805)467-3141

ISBN 9780615335537

Acknowledgments:

With appreciation and gratitude, I would like to thank the following people for their time, support, and hard work.

Cover photography: Drew Lassen
Cover model: Caitlin Lassen
Formatting and editing: Courtney Helland
Editing: Trine Marlen
Digital wizard: Jean Singer-West

I would also like to thank my lovely wife, Caren, for her patience, understanding, and constant encouragement.

INTRODUCTION

Before we saw them, we heard them. Dogs barking and the sound of hooves clicking on the pavement. Sheep bleating and baaaa-ing. It was a vast amount of noise coming up the hill. A shepherd was bringing up the rear, singing and whistling and clicking to his dog helpers. He was herding about 1500 sheep right up the middle of the street that fronts our restaurant! I'm not kidding. A regular "lamb jam" right out in the front of the Tenth Street Cafe. He had these three amazing, outstandingly athletic dogs. They were black and white Border Collies. One would scamper across the backs of the tightly bunched sheep, keeping them from going up the off ramp to Highway 101. The other two were moving all around the herd, driving and snapping and barking and moving all the sheep forward. It was really quite amazing to watch. We sat there mesmerized and surprised and enjoying ourselves immensely!

"Aganon" was the greeting the shepherd called to us as he waved his hand in a happy salute! We lifted our wine glasses as a return salute and offered him a glass of the ruby elixir. He was most delighted to share a glass of wine and offer his profound advice regarding our fledgling restaurant. He said to us "...you should do Basque food. It is the best cooking in the world. I have to drive 100 miles to find a Basque Restaurant."

I'm sorry I don't remember his name. I'm not good with names and his was difficult to pronounce, but I will never forget his genuine smile and simple advice. He finished his wine and thanked us, wished us well, and jogged off to catch up with his sheep and his dogs.

Basque Food? How off the wall was that? Surprisingly, and perhaps fortuitous, I happen to have Basque heritage that I have always enjoyed but never thought to focus a business around. I decided that it would indeed be fun to offer a Basque dinner on a few occasions to our wonderful customers and our many friends in the surrounding wine businesses.

We started by offering a Basque feast once a month. No menu, always chef's choice and one seating only. Well, to make a long story short, it took on a life of its own. We were running to keep up with it. We went from once a month to every Wednesday. Then we added Friday and Saturday. Finally we let go of our other menu and focused entirely on Basque food. Thus began the Tenth Street Basque Café, located in the middle of wine country on the Central Coast of California.

We are surrounded by amazing produce and farmer's markets that are full to overflowing. Fresh fish from the coast; beautiful fresh-from-the-tree fruits, just picked that morning; luscious strawberries and olallaberries; heirloom tomatoes of

every hue and stripe that are so sweet you can't believe it; lettuces of every variety; beets; baby carrots; green, white, and purple asparagus; kale and chard; and other stuff I don't even know what it is. Everything is grown locally and arranged and displayed in a kaleidoscope of bushel baskets and trays of fresh produce, nuts, and artisan breads. I'm spoiled rotten to have access to such wonderful ingredients and world-class wines. We have the privilege of offering a seasonal, market driven menu every single night!

It is with appreciation and gratitude that we offer you this book filled with what we have learned along the way creating food for our guests, friends, and family. The recipes in this book are not your normal restaurant offerings. Most restaurant cooking happens in about 15 minutes (providing all the prep work is done). The kind of cooking and the recipes offered here are more suited to home cooking where you have lots of time and can truly enjoy the process. It's the kind of cooking most of our grandmothers did daily.

We pride ourselves on creating and cooking with inexpensive simple things in an excellent manner and ending up with a divine dish. It is our intent to make this cookbook user friendly so you can make some of our most requested recipes at home. I have included lots of chef's hints and tips that no one ever tells you – and no one seems to write about it either. If you didn't learn it from someone, how would you know? We hope you find this book useful, a fun read, and that you find recipes you want to cook and enjoy with your family and friends.

AGANON!

Map of the Basque homeland

TABLE OF CONTENTS

This is not your mother's cookbook!

It is not a coffee table cookbook. There are no staged, pretty pictures from a professional food stylist. This is a working cookbook, designed to be used. Feel free to write in the margins. Make notes, change or add things, and by all means have fun. Remember, it's only food!

In this book you will find a sharing of tips, hints, anecdotes, professional secrets and tricks. It is filled with easy to prepare, world-famous recipes from Chef Dallas, executive chef and owner of the Tenth Street Basque Café, located in the heart of the wine country on the Central Coast of California.

Questions? Comments? Please feel free to contact Chef Dallas at thebasque-cafe@gmail.com. He'd love to hear from you!

Knives

Sharp is good. Dull is dangerous. More chefs and cooks are injured with dull knives, not sharp knives. That sounds so counter intuitive, but the reality is that a dull knife will slip off the cutting surface and the next step is the first aid kit.

Most restaurants employ a roving knife sharpening service to visit their kitchen periodically and sharpen all the knives for the kitchen crew. I like to take care of mine myself because I always know how sharp they really are. There are quite a few ways to keep your knives sharp, but I'm only going to discuss the way I do it because all the other ways are too scary for me.

We have all watched transfixed as a famous TV chef uses their steel to sharpen their knives. Their hands are a blur and it sounds like a medieval sword fight. A look of stern concentration knits their brow. If you have years to practice, nerves of steel, and the dexterity of an Olympic gymnast, I say go for it.

If you are more like me, a tad nearsighted and certainly not the most coordinated, try my own personal technique. I have already mentioned that knives are sharp and can be dangerous. I don't want you cutting something off you really wanted to keep.

What you will need:

- A Wet Stone
- A Diamond Honing Rod
- A Steel

These things you will have your entire life. You will carry them with you from kitchen to kitchen. Get nice ones. Get them at a good knife store. Knife stores are so cool. There are all kinds of interesting things and people in knife stores. Also, get a knife bag that rolls up; it's an easy way to keep your knives together when you cook someplace other than your own kitchen. Besides, when you show up with your own knives in a snazzy carrier, everyone gives you more respect.

Using the Wet Stone

Use a small amount of water to wet the stone. Hold the knife with the blade at about a 45 degree angle to the stone and gently push the blade of your knife away from you, across the stone in one direction. Pretend you are slicing off a <u>very</u> thin layer from the top of the stone. Turn the knife over and do it again – this time slicing the stone towards you. Repeat this process a couple of times. After a few runs with the knife over the stone you are ready for the next step.

Using the Honing Rod

If you are right handed, hold the knife in your right hand with the blade towards the floor and the honing rod in your left. Very gently, without applying any pressure, place the broad side of the blade on top of the honing rod and pull the entire length of the blade along the rod, moving from the top of the honing rod to the bottom as you pull. Note that the knife should be pretty flat against the honing rod - at about a 15 degree angle - while you pull it. Now repeat the process, but this time place the blade on the underside of the honing rod. Again, pull along the entire length of the blade, moving from the top of the honing rod to the bottom. In your minds eye, you are using the knife to cut very thin slices off the rod, just like with the wet stone. But this time do it even more gently as you are simply de-burring the microscopic imperfections caused after using the wet stone. Now steel yourself for the next step, pun intended....get it?

Using the Steel

Take an old cutting board and drill a small hole in it. (Or use one with a pre-drilled hole.) Place the pointy end of the steel in the hole. Take your knife and envision you are polishing the cutting edge by drawing it down the length of the steel from the guard to the cutting board. Repeat on the other side of the steel. Do not exert any pressure at all. The reason to use the steel is to even up the cutting edge of the knife so that it lines up straight. It takes very little effort or speed. Usually 5 or 6 pulls to align the blade is enough. You will notice an immediate difference in the sharpness of your knives. Think of this as being no different than tuning a piano or violin; everything just works better with a little tune up.

Chef's notes - My father was a merchant marine; he gave me the following advice. "Son" he said, "if you are ever in a shady bar, being harassed by a guy who doesn't have any hair on his forearm, run away. That is how he tests the sharpness of his knife; he tests it by shaving off the hair on his arm. It's probably a big nasty sharp one hiding in his pocket. Don't fight that guy, just get outta there." Dear old Dad didn't teach me much, but this particular tip did come in handy in Taiwan about a million years ago at a somewhat suspect establishment. Thanks, Dad.

Let's get back to kitchen knives. Here is a list of my favorites.

- Large chef's knife, 10"
- Medium chef's knife, 8 ½ "
- Boning knife
- Paring knife
- Carving knife
- Butcher's cleaver
- Bread knife with a serrated edge, and off-set handle, if you can find one

Most knives available to chefs today are stainless steel and made in foreign countries. Stainless steel knives are quite handsome but they are hard to sharpen

and difficult to keep sharp. You have to keep at them all the time with the stone, the honing rod and the steel. I know because I use them.

The best knives are actually the old knives they used back in the day. Look for them at yard sales, in the backs of barns, thrift stores, way in the back of a kitchen drawer, maybe your grandma's knife collection. Estate sales are usually a good hunting ground. Look for the rusty knives. Those are real steel, not stainless steel. Look at the handle. If the tongue of the blade goes all the way through, and the handle is secure and tight, that's the one you want. After you clean it up, it will become your favorite knife. A real steel knife gets the sharpest and it stays that way for a long while if you don't abuse it. Always cut on a cutting board, never on a counter top other than a butcher block.

These old steel knives take a little more work to care for, but they are well worth it. Always dry the blade after cleaning. Rub a little cooking oil down the blade and wipe dry with a kitchen towel to keep the rust at bay. Let me repeat myself, they take a little more effort to care for, but they are far superior to their mass produced stainless steel cousins of today.

Pots and Pans

Cast Iron

If this was radio, you would hear the sound of true awe in my voice. It gets hot quickly, stays hot, cooks evenly, and, finally, it's great for building upper body strength. They don't have to be those unattractive black things either (but those are the kind I use.) There is some imported porcelain clad cast iron cookware from France. The cookware costs an arm and a leg, but they cook great. There are some manufactured domestically right here in the good old United States. These work just as well as the import and cost a fraction of the price. Buy American.

The care and feeding of cast iron cookware is something no one ever teaches you because everyone is using those non-stick pans. This is another case where Grandma had the right idea. When you buy a black cast iron cooking piece, it needs to be seasoned before you can use it. When you get it home, wash it in hot soapy water. Dry it off. If it is a pot or a pan, place about 2 inches of cooking oil in it and place it in a cold oven, turn it on to about 250 degrees and leave it in there for about 2 hours. Remove it from the oven and drain off the oil. Wipe the pan with paper towels or dry it over an open flame on the stovetop until it is as dry as you can get it. Whenever you use it, be sure to dry it completely before you put it away or it will rust. If you pull it out to use and it has a little rust on it, just rinse it out, put some cooking oil on a paper towel and wipe away any surface rust. It should come right off and doesn't bother anything. Next time, just be sure it is very dry when you put it away and that it has a slight sheen of oil that has worked its way into the cooking surface. You can always rinse and dry it and rub some additional cooking oil in with paper towels just before you put it away. I like to hang mine on a pot rack so as to keep air circulating around them. If you find things begin to stick to the surface when you are cooking, try seasoning again. Sometimes you have to season two or three times before the pan becomes truly "non stick". Always

clean quickly in hot water, no soap. Do not ever soak it. If you do, be prepared to re-season your pan.

So, to summarize, in and out of hot water, rinse completely and dry immediately by placing over an open flame on the stove or dry thoroughly with paper towels. Don't use your nice dish towels; they will get black and oily. If you get porcelain clad cast iron, you do not have to season it.

Aluminum

At the restaurant we use aluminum stock pots and cooking pots. They aren't glamorous, but you can scrub the heck out of them and they cook great. Anodized aluminum pots and pans work well at home, but are too easily scratched in a commercial setting.

Stainless Steel

Most cooks at home use stainless steel cookware. They work great and they can be kept nice and shiny. Look for pans without plastic handles so you can put the pan and the lid in the oven. At home we use a stainless steel set with copper inlaid bottoms. They are pretty heavy duty and we like cooking in them, but they certainly are not practical for restaurant cooking. We use stainless steel hotel pans in different sizes for baking in the oven at the restaurant; same for the sheet pans.

Non Stick

Forget nonstick, except a couple of pans for an occasional grilled cheese sandwich or an omelet. Nonstick pans are inferior when it comes to real cooking: you just can't get the pan hot enough to sear food before you start having issues with the stuff they coat the pans with.

Copper

Love them. Nothing conducts heat better than copper. If you can afford them, by all means go for it. If you can only afford one, buy a sauté pan.

Tools

Here is a list of some of the tools and equipment I think every chef should have in their kitchen. Don't go out and buy them all at once. Simply start with your existing collection of tools and add more as you cook.

- Mortar and pestle – get the biggest you can lift
- Food processor – with an "S" blade, a shredding blade, and a slicing blade
- Emersion blender
- Counter stand mixer – with a dough hook, a mixing paddle, and a wire whisk. Get the kind of mixer where the head tilts back, it's just easier to use
- Metal tongs
- Metal long handled spoons, one slotted
- Micro planer
- Measuring cups – 1, 2, and 4 cup glass measuring cups and a stacking set with 1/4, 1/3, 1/2, and 1 cup
- Set of measuring spoons
- Stainless steel mixing bowls, 3 sizes that nest

- Hand fruit juicer
- Hand held potato masher
- Hand held electric mixer
- Electric knife
- Rice steamer
- Good oven mittens
- Chef's twine
- Kitchen scale – if you can't find a digital scale at the local kitchen supply store that won't break the bank, try the local office supply store. Look for a digital postal scale
- Cheese grater - buy the biggest bad boy you can find, the box type is best. Make sure it fits your hand and is easy to use. Your knuckles will thank you
- Colander
- Hand held strainer
- Blow torch - forget about a fancy crème brulee kitchen style torch, they are just too wimpy. Run down to your local hardware store and purchase a self igniting blow torch for half the price and twice the efficiency. As an added bonus, the guys in the kitchen will really enjoy using it
- Instant read thermometer – ever notice those little pockets on the left sleeve of chefs' coats? That's where the instant thermometer lives. This is one of the most important and handy gadgets that you can use. Don't guess if that steak is medium rare. Just give it a poke with the instant read and you will know immediately. Ain't technology grand?
- Remote thermometer probe – this is a great time saver when you only care about the temperature of one thing at a time. It's also handy when you don't want to continuously open the oven door to stick your meal with the instant read thermometer to check the internal temperature. Simply place the probe into the densest part of the meat before you start cooking and place the read-out outside of the oven, someplace easy to see. The probe monitors the internal temperature for you
- A heavy duty mandolin – don't buy the cheap one. You want one with a good hand guard and several different blades and settings. A good mandolin makes for very quick work when cutting coleslaw, slicing tomatoes, slicing zucchini or other squashes, and thinly slicing other vegetables
- Wooden spoons - you can never have too many of them. They work well on those non stick pans I told you to never use. They are great for turning things over in a skillet, stirring the soup, and they do a great job as attention getters for wayward children, pets, and spouses. When used for banging on a pot lid, they can get the attention of an entire restaurant
- Hand whisks – stainless steel ones, large and small. Don't get those plastic coated ones to be used in those bad non stick pans, they melt, lose their shape, and are impossible to use or clean
- Kitchen timer
- Coffee grinder – get two, one for coffee and one for spices

Chef's notes - Stop what you are doing right now. Go get some measuring spoons and a box of salt. Measure a teaspoon of salt and pour it into the palm of your hand. Look at it. See how much volume it uses up. Now do it again, only this time measure a tablespoon and repeat the process. Now put those spoons away and start measuring with your eye a little bit more - unless you are baking. When recipes call for a teaspoon of this spice or a tablespoon of that, just pour some into your hand and throw it into the mix. It will free you up and make cooking much more fun and certainly less intimidating. And always, always taste your way through whatever it is you are cooking, correct the spice and salt and pepper as you go. Enjoy the process. A little of this and a pinch of that - hey we don't need no stinking spoons!

If you are a new cook and just starting out, you will find that you can simply build a kitchen pantry as you go along. A few basic staples such as flour, oil, sugar, salt, eggs, milk, butter, yeast and miscellaneous spices is where you start. Do not store your spices next to your hot stove, even though it is convenient. Unless you are using them up within a month, keep them someplace cooler. The heat simply shortens their shelf life.

If you have been cooking for a while, clean your pantry out of anything that you haven't used in a year. No one ever wants to throw out their spices because they are so expensive to buy. Ok, well at least take the lids off and smell each and every one. If they no longer smell like what is on the label... throw it away! Once it loses its pungent aroma how could it affect your food?

If you have your own homemade jams, jellies and canned jars of food, make sure the labels are still attached and if not, out they go. Even though we do not get into canning in this cookbook I would like to say that canning is an art form unto itself.

Because there are so many different kinds of oils, spices, and vinegars, I'm only going to talk about the ones that are particular to this cookbook. As for spices, dried are generally more powerful than fresh - so if you are substituting one for the other, make sure you take that into consideration. Sometimes they simply are not interchangeable and only fresh or only dry work in a particular recipe.

Herbs & Spices

- *Allspice* - A small berry which mimics a mix of clove, cinnamon, nutmeg, and mace. Always used ground or crushed.

- *Balsamic Vinegar* - dark brown vinegar made from fermented white grapes aged in wooden barrels. It has a sweet note compared to other vinegars.

- *Basil* - Dried or fresh, this is a sweet aromatic spice which adds a lot of flavor to many dishes. Basil and tomatoes like each other on the palate. Some recipes call for dry and some fresh; they are not always interchangeable.

- *Bay Laurel* - A leaf from the Mediterranean laurel tree family. One of the main ingredients in a "bouquet garni."

- *Bouquet Garni* - A combination of aromatic spices, herbs, and roots. A traditional garni would be a sprig of thyme, sprig of parsley, and a bay leaf. But things like orange peel, onions, whole peppercorns and whole cloves, ingredients with a very pungent aroma find their way into boquet garni bags. It is used to flavor soups and sauces. Usually tied together with cooks twine, or tied up in a little cheese cloth bag for easy removal.

- *California Bay* - Similar to "bay laurel" but with a stronger flavor and aroma.

- *Capers* - Pickled unopened flower bud. Used primarily in sauces or as a garnish.

- *Cinnamon* - Fragrant inner bark from a tree in the Far East. Sweet smelling and most commonly used in desserts, but it often finds its way into savory dishes especially in Spanish, Middle Eastern and Indian cuisine. I like to buy the whole bark and grind it myself.

- *Cloves* - Dried buds from a variety of myrtle trees grown in the Far East. Usually used ground up, but sometimes the dried buds are used whole for different applications.

- *Coriander* - An aromatic plant, Chinese parsley. The seeds and dried leaves add a pungent flavor to foods.

- *Cumin* - A spice with a strong, slightly bitter flavor.

- *Curry Powder* - A blend of spices from India. Can be mild, sweet, or flaming hot.

- *Dill* - Dried, fresh, or seeds. An excellent herb used on fish or with vegetables.

- *Fennel* - Dried or fresh. Has a licorice flavor and aroma. Grows wild all over California where there is an ocean influence. The seeds as well as the root bulb can be used.

- *Ginger* - Fresh or dried. A spicy rhizome used for flavoring.

- *Horseradish* - A root, used either fresh or dried. Hot and spicy, adds punch to sauces and dishes.

- *Juniper Berries* - A small berry with strong pungent flavor and aroma of pine needles. Great for wild game dishes. Also, one of the flavorings used in gin.

- *Nutmeg* - A close cousin of mace with nutmeg being the stronger flavored and more aromatic. Can be used in both savory and sweet dishes.

- *Mint* - An herb easily grown in the garden or in a pot. It has a refreshing smell and flavor. Can be used dried or fresh, but fresh is much stronger.

- *Oregano* - Very easy to grow in a kitchen garden. Dried or fresh, it adds flavor to savory dishes. Loves tomatoes.

- *Olive Oil* - Don't get crazy. You really don't need expensive super duper double virgin olive oil pressed between the toes of angelic virgins. I like to use a blend of good ole canola oil and a good fragrant olive oil - 75% canola and 25% olive. (My favorites are made with Arbiquino olives). This blend gives you the ability to cook at a high heat. Olive oil alone has a much lower smoke point. With the blend you get the best of both worlds, the olive oil for flavor and aroma and the canola oil for its ability to cook at high heats.

- *Paprika* - Buy the regular kind. It can add a little spicy heat and color to food preparation. Not as hot as pepper. If your recipe calls for smoked Paprika, just heat some in a dry skillet over medium heat, stirring constantly on the stove top until it begins to release its oils and aroma. Remove from heat before it starts to smoke. Pay close attention because it can go from just starting to smoke to burnt in an instant.

- *Parsley* - Another candidate for your easy to grow kitchen garden. Flavorful and colorful it adds some to punch to whatever it is added to. Works great as a color contrast garnish.

- *Pepper* - Use coarse black pepper, or grind your own peppercorns. Many recipes call for white pepper, especially in white sauces. I only use coarse ground black pepper; if you can see it in the sauce, I like the way it looks. If you need a finer grain, use the mortar and pestle to crush the peppercorn seeds.

- *Rosemary* - Drought tolerant and easily grown. If you live in California, it's almost a weed. Very pungent either dried or fresh. Fabulous on just about any meat, chicken, or fish dish. Also great to infuse olive oil.

- *Saffron* - Buy the best. Look at it when you buy it, you want threads of saffron. Don't buy the ground up powder. Each one of the saffron threads is hand harvested from a crocus flower, most grown in Spain. It's expensive because the hand labor is huge. Whenever you cook with saffron, always make it into a kind of tea before you add it to what you are cooking. It dispenses the flavor better. Use it sparingly. Too much saffron can taste medicinal.

- *Sage* - Another herb that grows wild in the Western United States. Great for pork dishes and used in stuffing's. Its flavors are savory and mild.

- *Salt* - Always cook with Kosher or sea salt.

- *Soy Sauce* – Great for marinating meats and vegetables. Made from fermented soy beans.

- *Thyme* - Used by the Greeks in meat and vegetable dishes as well as for medicinal purposes. Less is best, add sparingly and taste as you go so as not to overpower the dish you are making.

- *Turmeric* - A peppery spice with a distinctive yellow color. Major component in prepared mustard to add color and flavor, also used in most curry powders.

- *Vanilla* - Most vanilla available today is a synthetic imitator of the real thing. Pure vanilla extract is available, it is more costly, but worth the price. Read the label, it will tell you if it is pure or imitation. Dried seed pods are also available, but harder to find.

- *Vinegar* - Can be either real or synthetic. This is one ingredient where the price usually reflects the quality.

Proteins

We are blessed with the most abundant variety and supply of proteins than at any other time in human history. Personally, nothing makes me happier than a big hunk of meat on the grill. I like to cook it and I like to eat it - arghhhhh. I guess it's a guy thing. Grilling usually requires a more expensive cut of meat or it can be tough.

Chicken

Old chickens have more flavor than young chickens. If you are in a hurry and need a chicken breast fast, younger is better, also much more expensive. If you have more time and you enjoy cooking, buy a big whole chicken or leg quarters of a chicken that is big. Bigger usually means older, you can cook it longer, it will taste better, and when it falls off the bone it is not mush. Unlike a young pullet, if you cook that for a long time it will become over cooked, dry, and tasteless. But with the older birds you will find they can be cooked longer and still have great texture and they taste like real chicken!

Beef

Inexpensive cuts work best when creating most of the recipes in this book. It's all about how it is prepared. Anyone can throw a steak on the grill and cook it pretty well. The techniques I am sharing with you here in this book usually require some time in the oven or in the stew pot.

Pork

It's all good. Pork chops, loin roasts, butts and shoulders, even the feet can be made into some real mouthwatering dishes. A pound of bacon is approximately 14 slices, that's just a little more than an ounce a strip. Sometimes we use bacon strips to wrap around other meats to impart some of that delicious fat to keep other leaner foods moist and tasty.

Fish

Buy local. If you live in the Midwest, buy ocean fish that has been flash frozen. Frozen fish that has always been handled properly, more times than not, is a better product than fish that has been only refrigerated and shipped a thousand miles. Wild fishes are usually firmer and tastier than farmed fish. Except catfish, farm raised catfish taste better than their wild brothers, they eat better.

Shrimp

I love shrimp. I sometimes even crave shrimp. However, and this is a big caveat, today's shrimp is all about location, location, location. Buy shrimp that is caught off the coast or raised in America. Most shrimp available today is from the Far East and is raised in dubious quality water. Large amounts of antibiotics are pumped into their habitat to keep them alive. I don't crave that kind of shrimp. Buy local, or flash frozen shrimp from anywhere in the USA or caught in the Gulf of Mexico. If I can't buy it from a source in the US, I make something else for dinner. It may cost a little more, but I feel good about helping to keep our shrimp industry alive and well here at home.

Whenever I buy any seafood or shell fish, I always ask my fish monger "Where does it come from." Always! Get to know your fish monger, he will let you know when some really quality product is available. Think of him as one of your MVP's on your cooking team. Find him by looking in the yellow pages under "Seafood" or call the best restaurant in town and ask them where they buy their fish. Most large grocery stores now also have a good fish market along with their butcher counter.

Eggs

If you can, buy free range eggs locally at your farmer's market. Free range means they run around in the sunlight in the hen yard, eating bugs, kitchen trimmings, as well as chicken feed and scratch. These eggs can cost a little more, but are well worth it. Eggs don't have to be refrigerated if you are planning on using them right away, within a week or so. In the refrigerator, eggs can keep a long time, but they begin to lose their quality and ability to make cakes rise nicely or custards that do not break.

You can tell if an egg is really fresh when you crack it open: if the egg yolk does not flatten out, i.e. it stays nice and perky, it's a fresh egg. If you are unsure about an egg, place it in a bowl of water; if it floats don't use it. If it stands on one end, you should probably use it soon. And don't dare crack it open it if it pops to the top like a bobber on a fishing line. Air gets inside through small pours in the shell and spoils the egg. Spoiled eggs are about as rotten a smell as there is.

Also, if you have never eaten free range chicken eggs, don't be alarmed when you crack it open and find a bright yellow yolk. I mean it is *really* yellow. Most eggs that come from egg ranches are a perfectly fine product, but their yolks are not nearly as yellow. In fact, I was once told that some chicken feed has red dye #2 in it to give the yolk some yellowish color at all. These chickens only eat chicken feed, no bugs, no ranch kitchen trimmings, no sunlight, and as a result, the yolks aren't as yellow. Don't freak out here - I use egg ranch eggs all the time, but it is a real treat to get to use fresh free range eggs. They are defiantly worth the price and are awesome in a number of dishes.

Al Dente	An Italian term indicating a desired texture and doneness in food. Usually used when describing pasta, but it applies to all foods except proteins. It depicts that the outside of something is tender yet the inside is still firm.
Bard	No, no, no, not William Shakespeare (the Bard). It means to wrap pieces of fat, bacon, or pork fat around leaner cuts of meat to keep them moist and to impart some additional flavor.
Baste	To spoon or brush pan drippings over food while it is cooking to enhance the color, flavor, and to prevent food from drying out. Melted butter or other marinades can also be used for basting.
Blanch	To plunge food into boiling water, usually fruits or vegetables, and then into cold water to stop the cooking process, retain color, and flavor. This is done to tenderize the ingredient so that is more pliable, like grape leaves for stuffing, or to help loosen skins on fruits and vegetables to ease the peeling process.
Clarified Butter	Butter that has been heated to separate the oil from the solids. When separated, the solids are discarded leaving behind clear butter oil that has a higher smoke point than regular butter. Also great for dipping lobster.
Confit	To immerse a food into a liquid or oil to impregnate that food with flavor and to help preserve it for later use. Before refrigeration, it was a preferred way to store food for an extended period of time.
Crush	Using the flat side of a wide knife, whack food to help release juices and oils.

Deglaze	After removing cooked food and most of the oil and pan-drippings from a roasting pan or skillet add liquid of choice (water, wine, juice, or stock) to loosen all those yummy crusty bits and pieces that are stuck to the pan. Using your trusty wooden spoon, scrape and coax and loosen all those stubborn pieces that don't want to let go. This will create a delicious base for a sauce to serve with whatever it is you just cooked. Also, you will find that deglazing cleans the pan well, making for an easier clean up later.
Chiffonade	Roll together leafy vegetables or herbs into a little cigar shaped roll. Slice across the roll in thin strips making very thin strips usually used for garnishing.
Dredge	To coat with flour before frying or cooking.
Double Bound	A more complicated method of dredging food that creates a tastier and thicker crust. Food is first coated with flour then dipped into whisked eggs, and then dipped into bread crumbs before cooking.
Egg Wash	Whole eggs that have been whisked together with a splash of water. Usually brushed onto other surfaces to aid in browning, especially on pie dough. It can also be used as "glue" to stick pieces of pastry together.
Emulsify	Slowly adding oil or fat to one liquid or ingredient to another while whisking continuously to thoroughly blend it all together.
Fold	Using a slow figure eight movement to mix one or more ingredients into another. It is a considerably more gentle way of incorporating ingredients without breaking down fragile foods or letting out all the air that had been previously created, like a meringue.
Glaze	To add sugar, honey, or other sweetener to the outer layer of cooked meat or baked dishes to impart a sheen or shine plus sweetness. An example would be a honey glazed ham.
Gluten	A protein found in wheat. It makes dough elastic and aids in trapping air when dough rises.

Infuse	Adding herbs or other flavorful ingredients to a liquid or oil. An example would be adding a rosemary sprig, or whole garlic, to a bottle of olive oil so as to give it a special flavor.
Knead	Manipulating dough by stretching and pushing it to develop gluten. Kneading helps trap air and gas released from yeast when making bread, thus making the dough lighter. Dough can be kneaded by hand, mechanically with a mixer and dough hook, or even in the food processor. If you do a lot of bread making by hand, you will get really buff.
Lard	Used the same way as Bard. A technique to promote moistness and flavor. An example would be to insert strips of bacon into game meats that are naturally very lean to lend some moistness and flavor. Animal fat that has been rendered and then re-solidified is also called lard.
Julienne	A French term meaning to slice vegetables into thin strips. "Matchsticks" would be an American term for the same thing.
Marinade	To submerge food into a liquid that imparts flavor and/or tenderizes.
Mirepoix	Celery, carrots and onions chopped finely and sautéed until caramelized. Used as a base for a number of dishes.
Nap	To pour gravy or sauce on the bottom of a plate or platter before placing the food on top. "Nap the plate."
Pulse	To use the food processor in short bursts of chopping or mixing.
Parboil	To partially cook in boiling water.
Puree	To reduce food to a paste. An example would be baby food.

Reduce	To minimize by heat the volume of a liquid. Boiling allows steam to escape and reduces the amount of liquid while intensifying the flavor. The water evaporates from the liquid leaving a lesser amount with more flavor. Reducing a liquid concentrates its flavor.
Rest	Letting cooked food sit for a few minutes before cutting. Letting meat rest before carving allows the juices to re-solidify and not run out when cut.
Roux	A fat and flour combination used to thicken soups, sauces, and stews. It also adds flavor layers.
Rub	A dry marinade made from ingredients that allow you to rub it all over and into meat, poultry, or fish. It imparts flavoring and promotes tenderizing. Best if rubbed and refrigerated overnight. Great on pork ribs.
Skim	To remove from the top of something else, usually fats, grease or foam from a liquid. Foam is easily removed with a ladle, fats are a little harder. The best method is to partially submerge a ladle into the hot liquid wherein the fat has risen to the surface; it will separate and flow into the ladle. It can be a long process to remove all the fat from something. Another, and much easier, way to do it is to refrigerate for several hours (overnight is better) whatever it is you are trying to separate fat from, like chicken stock. All the fat will float to the top. It will solidify and then can be easily removed.
Spray Oil	Vegetable/cooking oil in a spray bottle.
Tapas	Spanish appetizers. The little dishes of Spain.
Tenderize	Beating the heck out of a tougher cut of meat with a meat mallet. Also to pierce the meat many times to compromise the connecting tissue or to submerge in a marinade.
Water bath	Placing a smaller container to be cooked into a larger container that is partially filled with water, so as to cook indirectly in boiling water. It keeps fragile foods, like custards, from sticking to the pan, burning, curdling and drying out.

Whisk	Vigorously beating a liquid to help emulsify and/or to incorporate air. Hand mixers, whisks, food processors, and even a dinner fork can be used to whisk.
Zest	The outside rind of an orange, lemon or lime that has been removed with a micro planer or knife. Be careful to only remove the skin, the colored part, of the skin. The white membrane just beneath can be bitter.

Albacore Fishcakes

Makes about (20) 2" cakes or 4 large patties

3 6-oz cans water packed, light albacore tuna	*1 egg, whisked lightly*
¾ cup coarsely chopped bread crumbs	*1 rib celery, finely diced*
½ cup shredded parmesan cheese	*1 large zucchini, shredded*
	Spray Oil

Preheat oven to 350 degrees.

Into a large mixing bowl, place tuna including water from the can. The water from the can adds flavor as well as liquid to moisten the dish. Add all other ingredients and mix well.

On a cookie sheet, place parchment paper and spray a fine mist of cooking oil overall. Using a #24 (1 ½ oz) ice cream scoop, make fish balls about the size of a golf ball. Place the fish balls on the parchment paper lining the cookie sheet, spaced apart and not touching. Flatten each fish ball slightly with the palm of your hand. The cheese will melt a little bit and you don't want them to melt together so be sure they have a little space between them. Cook for about 15 - 20 minutes. Every oven is different, so test for doneness by looking at the bottom of one of the fish cakes. It will have browned moderately when done. Luckily, fishcakes are very forgiving - it's pretty hard to burn them. Nicely browned on the bottom and served hot with a zesty sauce topper they are yummy!

Choose one of the sauces in this book to top these delicious Tapas. Personally, I like the artichoke, pesto, mushroom sauce (see page 64).

These tasty little morsels can also be made in various sizes depending on how you want to serve them. We have made them the size of a hamburger patty and served as a main dish, or we make them bite sized like a cookie and served with a tangy sauce as a Tapas dish. The smaller size is great at a party because they can be served to your guests as finger food.

Because these are "oven fried" the cook can place them in the oven and do something else! We also like this method for cooking potato pancakes. The cook is not chained to the stove making sure the cakes don't burn and you don't have to turn them over. This method also eliminates a lot of oil that is usually found when they are fried on the stove top. When cooked on the stove top, after frying you have to place them on a paper towel to wick off excess oil. Oven frying eliminates this because only a small amount of oil is sprayed onto the parchment paper.

Chef's notes - You can substitute crab meat or salmon to make these little cakes. If you are using meats that are not canned, you need to add a little water or stock to the mix to make it all stick together.

Here's another hint. Use a pizza stone in your oven. Place the cookie sheet with these little fish cakes directly on top of the pizza stone to help them brown up real nice on the bottom. Make sure they are cooked all the way through. You don't want them mushy in the middle. The bottoms of the fish cakes should have turned to a golden brown when finished.

Asparagus Wrapped with Prosciutto
Serves 4 to 6

1 lb bunch pencil thin asparagus	*½ cup balsamic vinegar*
¼ lb thinly sliced Prosciutto	*Salt and pepper to taste*

Preheat oven to 350 degrees.

Take each piece of asparagus and snap off bottom portion which is tough. It will naturally break off where it begins to become tender. Wrap each piece of asparagus with a slice of Prosciutto and place on a cookie sheet and lightly spray with your favorite olive oil. Sprinkle lightly with salt and cracked pepper. Bake in 350 degree oven for 15 minutes. Do not overcook; you don't want them to be limp.

Reduce balsamic vinegar by half over medium heat. Drizzle the thickened vinegar syrup over the cooked Prosciutto wrapped asparagus.

Can be served hot or cold.

Basque Potatoes
Serves 6

4 medium unpeeled Russet potatoes	*2 Tbs cooking oil*
1 large peeled yam	*Pinch of red pepper flakes*
1 ½ Tbs paprika	*1 tsp salt*
1 tsp onion powder	*½ cup mayonnaise*
1 tsp garlic powder	*4 tsp chopped garlic*
½ tsp coarse ground black pepper	

Preheat oven to 350 degrees

Wash Russet potatoes and cut into bite sized pieces. Peel and cut yam into bite sized pieces. Place yams and potatoes into baking dish and add the oil.

Mix together the paprika, onion and garlic powder, coarse ground black pepper, red pepper flakes, and salt into a spice mixture. Sprinkle the spice mixture over the yams and potatoes, and then fold everything together making sure all the potatoes and yams are well coated with the oil and spices. Cover and bake in the oven at 350 degrees for 1 ¾ hours.

After you remove potatoes and yams from the oven, add mayonnaise and chopped garlic and fold everything together well. Transfer potatoes to serving platter and serve as a Tapas or as a side dish. Serve hot.

Chef's Notes - I truly cannot count how many times people have asked for the Basque potato recipe. If I don't make it one night, I'm hearing about it! Make this spice mixture in a triple recipe, or more, and store it in a jar to use each time you cook these wonderful spicy spuds. This recipe will become your favorite potato dish. I use whatever potato is in season, which is when they are at the peak of flavor. But you can't make it without the yams and get the creaminess that only yams bring to the table.

Carrot Soufflé
Serves 4

1 lb carrots	1 cup half and half cream
1 Tbs salt	Freshly shaved nutmeg
Water to cover carrots	Pinch of coarse black pepper
1 yellow onion, diced	2 Tbs Madeira or Tawny Sherry
1 Tbs roux (see page 57)	2 eggs, separated

Preheat oven to 350 degrees.

Shred carrots using the shredding blade of your food processor. Place carrots and salt in a medium sauté pan and add water until carrots are just covered. Cook over medium heat. Bring to a boil then reduce heat and simmer until carrots are well cooked and tender. Drain well. Place in food processor with the "S" steel blade and puree carrots, add the diced onions and process until smooth.

In heavy-bottomed sauce pan, add the roux to the cream. Cook over medium heat until the sauce begins to thicken. Using a micro planer, shave some whole nutmeg seed (2 to 3 passes) into the thickened cream, add the pepper, then add the Madeira or sherry. Remove the pan from the heat.

Separate the eggs. Whisk the yolks slightly. Slowly add some of the hot cream mixture, one table spoon at a time, into the whisked eggs, stirring continuously. (Adding the hot cream mixture slowly into eggs first keeps the eggs from cooking or curdling). Now add this mixture back into the remainder of the hot, thickened, and spiced cream. Fold together with the carrot and onion puree, gently mix together well, then allow to cool.

Meanwhile, whisk the egg whites until stiff. Gently fold into carrot mixture. Do not over mix. Pour into 4 buttered individual 1 cup soufflé dishes, or into a large buttered 4 cup soufflé dish. Create a water bath: place the ramekins or soufflé dish into a pan of water ¾ of the way up the dish and bake at 350 degrees for about 30 to 35 minutes. They are done when a tooth pick gently inserted comes out clean. The small ramekins may take less time to cook than one big one. Check at about 20 minutes. Resist the temptation to check on them too often. Each time you open the oven door the temperature drops and you run the risk of your dish deflating.

Garnish with crème fraische or sour cream.

Chickpeas with Cilantro and Lime
Serves 8

1 Tbs clarified butter	*¼ cup chicken stock (see page 38)*
4 garlic cloves, crushed	*¼ cup diced red pepper, seeded, skins removed*
1 tsp dry red pepper flakes	*¼ cup cilantro lime sauce (see page 61)*
1 cup diced tomatoes	
4 cups of canned chickpeas, drained	*Salt and pepper to taste*

Heat butter in a large skillet. Add garlic, red pepper and chopped tomato until cooked. Add chickpeas and sauté until heated thoroughly. Add chicken stock, red pepper flakes, and cilantro lime sauce and simmer for approximately 10 minutes. Serve hot with fresh bread.

This is also a nice complimentary side dish for lamb. It can be made into a wonderful dip by pulsing in a food processor until it is a rich paste. Perfect for dipping chips or topping bread. It is similar in texture to humus and can be interchangeable with recipes calling for humus.

Confetti Rice Mold
Serves 6

1/2 small white or yellow onion, peeled and diced	*1 pound fresh or frozen chopped spinach*
6 Tbs of butter	*½ cup chopped red bell pepper*
2 cups of uncooked long grain rice	*2 Tbs chopped garlic*
4 cups of boiling water	*Salt and pepper to taste*
2 quarts of boiling water	

Preheat oven to 350 degrees.

Melt 4 Tbs of butter on medium heat in a heavy-bottomed pan. Add the onions and cook until the onions are just translucent, about 5 to 6 minutes. Add the rice and cook and stir until the rice begins to become translucent. Do not brown the rice. All the rice should be coated with the butter. Add 4 cups of boiling water and a pinch of salt; cover and let simmer until all the water is absorbed and the rice is al dente, takes about 18 to 20 minutes.

In the meantime, clean and chop the spinach, removing any large stems (they are tough) or defrost a pound of chopped spinach. Drop spinach into 2 quarts boiling water and cook for about 5 minutes. Whether fresh or frozen, when just heated through, remove and drain water from spinach. Press any remaining water from the spinach with the back of a spoon or your hands. It should be relatively

dry. Combine the spinach, chopped red bell pepper, and the rice with the remaining 2 Tbs of butter. Toss thoroughly. Pack into a well-buttered 6 cup mold or oven-proof glass bowl, or make 6 one cup buttered oven proof ramekins for individual servings. Top each container with parchment paper cut to fit. Set cups or mold in pan with 2 or 3 inches of water (water bath) and bake at 350 degrees for about 15 -20 minutes. Remove from oven, remove parchment paper, and invert onto serving platter. Gently remove the mold. Serve hot with a citrus sauce on the side, (see page 62).

This is a very colorful dish as is. Its name comes from the fact that it looks like confetti on your plate! In the summertime, when I have access to fresh summer corn, I will barbeque some corn, cut it from the cob, and add it to the rice with the spinach and red bell pepper. It's beautiful served as a side dish or on its own as a Tapas.

Creamed Spinach
Serves 6

2 lbs fresh or frozen chopped spinach	½ tsp ground clove
½ - 2/3 cup whole milk	2 Tbs roux (see page 57)
¼ cup sugar	

Cook the spinach in a saucepan over medium heat. If using fresh spinach, cook until it is hot and completely wilted. If using frozen, cook until hot through and through, do not overcook or it will lose its nice green color. Overcook it and the color starts to darken and the flavor changes as well.

Drain water from spinach, you want it as dry as you can make it. I place cooked spinach in a strainer under cold running water first, pressing the water out of it when it is cool enough to handle. Place the roux, milk, clove, and sugar in a sauce pan over medium heat. Cook until thickened.

When cooked to a creamy consistency, add chopped cooked spinach. Use emersion blender to mix well until it is the desired consistency, similar to cooked oatmeal. The blender will continue to chop the spinach, and it will get creamier and creamier as you process. Some people like it really smooth and creamy. I usually serve it much chunkier as I think it gives it a more rustic texture. So just give it a few quick wizes with the wizzer and there you are.

To really bump up the flavor, you can add crispy chopped bacon as a topper to the spinach. To serve as a Tapas (little Spanish appetizer), place ½ cup of creamed spinach on a small plate and top with 4 slices of cooked bacon, or cooked Spanish chorizo sliced on the diagonal and fanned across a bed of creamed spinach. It is a beautiful and delicious side dish as well.

Chef's notes - I rarely use heavy cream when cooking. I think whole milk with the addition of the roux, which is half butter, is certainly rich enough. However, if you are really going over the top with this one, by all means, use heavy cream instead of whole milk.

Fried Cheese with Cilantro Lime Sauce
Serves 4

1 lb queso fresco cheese *¼ cup cooking oil*	*1 cup Cilantro Lime Sauce (see page 61)*

Cut cheese into ½ inch thick strips and refrigerate until ready to fry. In a skillet, heat a few tablespoons of oil until sizzling hot. (Drop a few drops of water into the skillet when you think it is hot enough, it pops when it is ready). Place several pieces of the cold cheese into the skillet and quickly sauté on each side until browned. Add more oil as needed. Plate and serve with the cilantro lime sauce drizzled over the top of each piece. Serve immediately. This dish makes a super easy Tapas and is always a hit.

Garlic Mashed Potatoes
Serves 6

4 medium Russet potatoes, unpeeled, cut into 2 inch pieces *2 Tbs chopped garlic*	*1 tsp salt* *3 Tbs room temperature butter* *½ cup whole milk*

Heat salted water to boiling. Add cut potatoes (they cook faster in smaller sizes, if the chunks are too big - like a whole half of a potato - the outside is cooked before the center). Cook for about 15 minutes, or until fork tender.

The potatoes need to be cooked enough for a hand masher to easily mash them. If you are unsure, take out a few and try to smash them. If they won't smash easily, cook them a few minutes longer. When cooked, drain out the water and put the potatoes back in the same pan. Mash while they are still hot, it is much harder to do when they cool. Add the milk, garlic, pinch of salt and the butter and mix thoroughly. TASTE them. Add salt and pepper to taste.

Leaving the skins on the potatoes gives them a rustic look that we like. They are probably more nutritious that way as well. Using only a potato masher we smash them just enough so that the end results are a little chunkier. If you want a really smooth whipped potato, peel the potatoes before you cook them. After they are cooked, using a hand held mixer, whip until smooth and creamy. Don't over whip them - they can get pasty.

Chef's notes - Wasabi or horseradish can be substituted or added to the garlic mashed potatoes resulting in more heat and a unique flavor.

Honey Glazed Carrots
Serves 4

1 lb carrots, peeled, cut on the bias in 1 inch pieces	1 tsp chopped garlic
½ cup honey	1 Tbs chopped fresh parsley
¼ pound unsalted butter	Salt and pepper to taste

Cook cut carrots in a covered microwave bowl for approximately 10 minutes or until fork tender. While carrots are cooking, heat the honey, butter and garlic over medium heat. Drain carrots and add to the honey glaze and toss. Salt and pepper to taste and garnish with the chopped parsley. If you are feeling creative, you can add sliced nuts, raisins or dried fruits. Go a little crazy and have some fun.

Lentil Stuffed Grape Leaves
Makes 20 servings

20 young grape leaves with stems removed	Pinch of salt
Juice and zest from one lemon	2 cups water
3 large tomatoes fire roasted with skins and seeds removed (or 1 14-oz can chopped tomatoes with juice)	2 cloves crushed garlic
	½ medium diced onion
	1 Tbs very good olive oil
1 cup green lentils	1 lemon for garnish

Preheat oven to 350 degrees.

Blanch grape leaves until pliable and easy to fold without snapping the skins or veins, approximately 3 to 5 minutes. Remove from the water and immediately place in a bath of ice water to stop the cooking process and fix the color.

Cook at a slow boil, 1 cup of lentils with 2 cups salted water for approximately 10 to 15 minutes, or until the lentils are just tender. Check often. Drain and set aside.

Sauté in oil the tomatoes, onions, and garlic until heated through, add cooked lentils, set aside to cool.

To assemble, take a cooled, blanched grape leaf and lay flat on prep surface, with the vein side up. Place a well rounded teaspoon of the lentil mixture near the bottom of the grape leaf near where the stem was. Fold grape leaf up from the bottom and then over from the sides (like a burrito) and then finish rolling and

folding over the stuffing mixture until you have a small cigar shaped roll. Place, seam-side down, in shallow baking dish. Continue until all the grape leaves and filling are used up or until the baking dish is full. Add enough water so there is about ½ inch in the bottom of the baking dish. Spray the top of the leaves with olive oil. Cover and bake ½ hour at 350 degrees. Drain. Cool. Arrange on serving platter, squeeze lemon juice over all and garnish with lemon wedges.

> Chef's notes - Any stuffing you like can be used. Experiment a little. We have made these with lamb and rice for a more traditional savory grape leaf. We have also made them in a savory/sweet style by adding dried fruit (raisins, chopped dried apricots, chopped dried dates) a little sugar and rice. Be creative, be brave. It's just food.

Migas
Serves 4

6 pieces raw bacon	¼ cup whole peeled garlic cloves
2 cups day old bread crumbs, coarsely chopped	1 chorizo sausage or ¼ lb bulk chorizo
1 chopped yellow onion	

Chop bacon into 1 inch pieces. Place in heavy skillet or cast iron pan. Squeeze chorizo sausage from casing, or use bulk chorizo, into same pan. Begin cooking over medium heat until fat is rendered from the bacon and the chorizo. When bacon is cooked medium well, add onions and garlic and cook until onions and garlic are tender and lightly browned.

Remove from heat. Add bread crumbs (make your own bread crumbs, as you want them very coarse, not fine). Throw day old or stale bread into your food processor and pulse until the bread is coarsely chopped. If it is too fine it will turn into paste. You want it to be the same consistency as stuffing that you have with your turkey dinner.

In the Basque country, Migas is served for breakfast, lunch, or dinner. It is great as a side dish and is delicious scrambled together with eggs, and sometimes it is served as a main course. The word "Migas" actually means breadcrumbs and it speaks to the frugal nature of Basque cuisine, where nothing is wasted.

Olive Tapenade
Makes 2 cups

One cup seeded black olives	1 Tbs chopped garlic
One cup pimento-stuffed green olives	¼ cup good quality olive oil

Combine all ingredients in food processor and pulse several times until everything is uniformly chopped like a relish. Be careful not to over process or the Tapenade will turn into a paste. If it does, not to worry, it will still be a great spread for bread or crackers, but it looks better when it is a little chunkier.

Serve as a spread on crackers or bread, and then get out of the way.

Red Bell Pepper and Eggplant Terrine

Serves 6

2 large eggplants	½ cup good quality olive oil
8 large red bell peppers, fire roasted, seeds and membrane removed	6 cloves garlic crushed, peeled, and minced
2 Tbs smoked paprika	Salt and pepper to taste

Preheat oven to 400 degrees.

Thinly slice the eggplants into ¼ inch disks and arrange them in a single layer on paper towels. Sprinkle salt on the eggplant. The paper towels will wick away quite a bit of moisture brought out by the salt. Removing moisture from the eggplant will allow it to cook without falling apart. Let the salted eggplant rest for about an hour before brushing off the salt.

Cut the peppers in half and arrange skin-side up on a baking sheet. Place in a very hot 400 degree oven. Cook until the skin of the peppers starts to blister, about 10 minutes. Remove the peppers, cool a little bit (so they don't melt the plastic), and then place into a large plastic freezer bag. Rub the peppers and the skins will easily be removed. Remove and discard the seeds, stems, and skins. Some of the blackened skin will stubbornly remain attached. Ignore it as it will add a wonderful flavor all its own. Cut the peppers into thick strips. Set aside.

In a dry skillet over medium heat, toast 2 Tbs paprika until it just begins to smoke, releasing the oil. Be very watchful so the paprika does not burn. Set aside.

Over a high heat, lightly coat a heavy frying pan with oil and quickly sauté the eggplant in batches, until browned on both sides. Oil will need to be added as you brown the eggplant, but add sparingly. Brown the eggplant quickly. Its natural tendency is to absorb the oil, so sauté quickly over high heat. You are just browning the outside.

Place browned eggplant, in one layer only, onto paper towels to absorb any excess oil. Now, in the same cooking skillet, add the smoked paprika, garlic, salt and pepper. Cook lightly, enough to soften the garlic halves. Then, with the back of a wooden spoon, mash the garlic into the oil and spices, forming a garlicky paste, set aside to cool.

Line a loaf pan, sides and bottom, parchment paper that has been cut to fit. Lightly spray the paper with oil. Place a layer of eggplant onto the oiled paper in the loaf pan. Place a layer of red peppers on top of the eggplant. Continue layering, alternating between eggplant and peppers. Make sure to press each layer together tightly.

When the final layer of eggplant is placed on top, brush on the garlicky oil paste. Use all of it. Place the loaf pan in a 350 degree oven for approximately 30 minutes. Remove and let cool. Cover with plastic wrap. Place a weight on top of the loaf to press down on all the layers. A similarly-sized loaf pan filled ½ way with water works well, but anything that has some weight and will fit the loaf pan so as to compress the vegetable layers overnight in the refrigerator also works.

The next day, remove the weight, and the plastic wrap. Invert the terrine onto a serving platter. It should slip right out. If not, run a knife around the edges and place it back onto the serving dish and invert once again. Give it a good thump to help it release. Leave the loaf pan on, helping the terrine hold its shape until serving time.

Just before serving, remove the loaf pan mold, including the parchment paper. Slice the Terrine. Let the first two or three pieces shingle down on the serving platter to show off the beautiful red and white stripes. Serve cold and sliced with an accompanying sauce of garlic aioli or crème fraische.

Red White and Bleu Potatoes

Makes 20 to 30 servings

10 -15 small new red potatoes	*1 cup mayonnaise*
3 pieces crispy bacon, crumbled	*2 Tbs cream cheese*
½ cup bleu cheese crumbles	*Salt and pepper to taste*

Cook potatoes in salted boiling water until fork tender. Do not overcook, you want them al dente. Remove from heat, drain, and submerge in cold water. This will stop the cooking process as well as set the color of the red potatoes. When they are cool enough to handle, slice a little bit off the bottom and top, and then cut in half. Each potato half should sit flat on a plate. With a small spoon or strawberry huller, hollow out a little well in the middle of each halved potato.

While the potatoes are cooking, place other ingredients into the food processor and give several short bursts until the ingredients are blended but still somewhat chunky. Place this mixture into a one gallon plastic bag. Cut off one corner of the plastic bag –creating a small hole in the bag. Note that the hole needs to be big enough to allow the blue cheese and bacon to pass through. Holding the bag like a pastry bag, roll down the top to remove most of the air and squeeze the filling through the opening and into each potato well. Arrange onto a serving platter and get out of the way. These are a hit as a Tapas. They are great at a cocktail party too. Your guests can pick one up and it is bite sized enough to be a one or two bite tasty little finger food. This is an obvious choice around the 4th of July.

Roasted Veggie Medley

Serves 6

1 onion, skin removed, thickly sliced in rounds	1 cup canola oil (use this kind of oil because it has a high smoke point)
1 red bell pepper, seeds removed, sliced into ½ inch strips	¼ cup extra virgin quality olive oil
	¼ cup chopped fresh cilantro
1 sliced zucchini, skin on, sliced length wise	1 tsp dry sweet basil
1 eggplant, skin on, sliced in rounds	1 tsp salt
1 Portobello mushroom, sliced into strips	1 tsp pepper
	1 tsp paprika
½ cup whole peeled garlic	1 tsp dry granulated garlic
2 Tbs vinegar	

Place all ingredients in a one-gallon zip lock plastic bag. Put in refrigerator for at least one hour. Turning frequently to make sure everything gets evenly coated. Overnight is even better.

Roast the marinated vegetables over hot coals on a barbeque, or over a gas grill (use a fish basket so you can flip everything easily without losing the veggies between the grates). Or you can place on a cookie sheet, and place below your oven broiler. Roast until the onions begin to blacken. Arrange on a large platter and serve hot or cold.

Chef's note - In the summertime, use any squash in season. I especially love the colorful addition of yellow crook necks and the funny shape of the patty pans. In the wintertime, I will par boil carrots and yams to replace the summer squash and treat them the same way. Do what makes you happy.

Spicy Nut and Date Balls
Makes 16 balls

1 cup coarsely chopped unsalted nuts	*½ cup fresh cilantro*
2 cloves garlic, peeled and crushed	*1 lime - zested and juiced*
1 piece peeled ginger, about the size of your thumb	*1 cup vegetable cooking oil*
	2 cups cooked long grain rice
¼ tsp dry turmeric	*¾ cup Diablo Sauce for dipping (see page 63)*
1 Tbs sugar	
1 Tbs soy sauce	*16 pitted dried dates*
1 tsp dry ginger	

You can use a variety of nuts for this recipe. I like hazelnuts, macadamias, almonds, peanuts, and/or pecans. Mix several together, your choice, just be sure to select the unsalted kinds.

Place garlic and ginger in food processor and pulse several times until well combined and minced. Add the turmeric, sugar, soy sauce, dry ginger, cilantro, lime juice and zest. Process until a paste is formed. Add 1 cup of the cooked rice and continue processing until the rice is incorporated into the original paste. Do not over process.

Place everything from the food processor into a mixing bowl and add the remaining cup of rice and mix thoroughly. Form the rice mixture around a date, making into balls about the size of a walnut, roll in chopped nuts. Refrigerate for about an hour. Heat 1 Tbs cooking oil in heavy skillet over medium high heat and fry the rice balls, turning them quickly onto all sides until golden brown all over. Add cooking oil as needed.

An alternate cooking method is to put the rice balls on a sheet pan lined with parchment paper, spray the balls with cooking oil and cook in a 400 degree oven until the rice balls are browned. Use an instant read thermometer and remove from the oven or the frying pan when the internal temperature reaches 130 degrees.

The fried ones from the stovetop are a little more decadent, but you can make a lot more of them at a time in the oven if you are feeding several guests. Serve warm or at room temperature.

Stuffed Artichokes
Serves 4

4 large artichokes	*2 Tbs chopped fresh parsley*
1 cup bread crumbs	*1 stick butter, melted*
3 cloves finely chopped garlic	*½ cup olive oil*
1/2 cup grated Parmesan cheese	*Salt and pepper to taste*

Clean and trim the artichokes. Submerge first in salted water to float out any debris or insects that may still be hiding between the leaves. Let the artichokes sit in the salt bath for about 20 minutes.

Cut away and discard any of the tougher leaves located at the bottom near the stem. With a very sharp knife, cut away about ¼ of the artichoke top. With kitchen scissors, cut away the thorny top of each leaf exposed on the surface of the artichoke. Most of the thorny tips have been cut away from the inside by taking off the top quarter.

Cut the bottom of the artichoke off so that it will sit flat on a plate. Save the stem portion, paring off the stringy fibers, to be cooked when you cook the rest of the artichoke. The stem is similar to the heart that remains in the artichoke. Some people think that this is the best part.

As you finish each artichoke, drop it into a bowl of water with lemon juice added (fresh lemon or bottled lemon juice is fine) to keep the artichokes from discoloring and oxidizing.

Parboil the artichokes in a large pot of salted water, 10 - 15 minutes. Be careful not to overcook the artichokes.

Drain upside down and cool. When cooled, gently spread apart the leaves and pull out the very middle cone of the artichoke. Discard these leaves and expose the fuzzy "choke" part of the vegetable. With a grapefruit spoon (One of those spoons with a serrated edge) or a teaspoon, scrape out the middle fuzzy chokes. Be careful not to scoop out the tender heart located at the bottom of the choke. When you're done, you should have a scraped area about the size a 50-cent piece.

Mix together the breadcrumbs, melted butter, Parmesan cheese, chopped parsley, and chopped garlic. Spoon the stuffing mixture into the middle part you just cleaned out and into as many of the outer leaves as you can without destroying the shape of the artichoke.

Now place the artichokes, stuffed and upright, into a large pot or deep baking dish with about an inch of water at the bottom. Each artichoke should sit upright in the bottom of the pan. Drizzle extra virgin olive over all the artichokes; be generous. Cover tightly with a lid or foil and cook either on the stovetop or in a preheated 350 oven for 35 minutes. Test for doneness by trying to remove one of the outer leaves, if it lets go easily, it is done. If it won't let go, cook a little longer, and test every 10 minutes.

We like to serve this dish at the restaurant sans any meat and offer it to our vegetarian guests as their entrée. If you choose to add some kind of ground protein

(beef, turkey, pork, lamb, chicken) you can serve this as a main dish. Brown any ground meat in a skillet and then mix into the breadcrumb mixture just prior to stuffing.

Stuffed Mushrooms

Serves 5 – 6

1 cup coarse-cut bread crumbs	*1 Tbs chopped garlic*
1/2 cup shredded Parmesan cheese	*10 - 12 large button white or brown mushrooms*
2 Tbs dried parsley	*¾ stick butter*

Preheat oven to 350 degrees.

Melt the butter in the microwave, add garlic, mix and set aside.

In the food processor, add breadcrumbs, cheese, and parsley, pulse 3 or 4 times. Be careful not to get the breadcrumbs too fine or they get pasty and don't cook as well. Stuff each mushroom with the breadcrumb mixture. Place stuffed mushrooms onto a shallow baking pan or cookie sheet with a lip. Place them close together, they cook better, and put about a teaspoon of the melted butter and garlic on each one. Drizzle enough butter on each mushroom so that some butter overflows onto the pan. A little butter in the bottom of the pan is necessary so the mushrooms can oven fry. Place in a preheated 350 degree oven. Cook for about 15 or 20 minutes. They are done when the breadcrumbs turn a little toasty and the butter on the bottom of the pan is bubbling. Serve hot.

Trust me, no matter how many you make, it will never be enough.

Three Peppers and Potato Tortilla

Serves 6

2 lbs Yukon potatoes, unpeeled, sliced thinly	*1 red bell pepper, sliced in ribbons*
1 medium red onion, peeled and diced	*1 green bell pepper, sliced in ribbons*
4 cloves garlic, peeled and crushed	*1 yellow bell pepper, sliced in ribbons*
1 Tbs paprika	*2 Tbs cooking oil*
4 Tbs parmesan cheese	*1 dozen eggs, whisked*

Heat the cooking oil in a large skillet on medium high heat. When the oil is hot, add the potato slices and cook until browned. Remove from the pan and set aside. In the same pan, cook the garlic and the pepper strips. Add the paprika and half of the diced onions. Cook until the peppers are al dente. Remove from the pan and keep with the cooked potatoes. Add the whisked eggs to the skillet. Lower the heat to a medium heat. Now pretend you are making a giant omelet. With a wood-

en spoon keep pulling the cooked egg away from the sides of the pan, back towards the middle, tipping the pan to allow gravity to send the uncooked egg into the space created. Repeat this process until the eggs are cooked. Add the cooked potatoes and pepper strips over the entire egg custard. Now sprinkle the Parmesan cheese over entire egg dish and then top with the remaining diced red onions.

This is the best part, get out your trusty blow torch. (Picture me with a big toothy grin. I get a thrill out of even saying that - blow torch. If there is a guy in the house, he will love helping you with this part.) Torch the top of the tortilla until the cheese melts and starts to brown. Use high heat, or you can place the egg dish under the broiler, until cheese starts to bubble and brown. Let rest for about ½ hour. Cut into pie shaped wedges and serve warm with a dollop of crème fraische, or sour cream.

Tuna Mousse
Serves 6 – 8

2 cans of water packed albacore white meat tuna, drained	4 green, pimento, stuffed olives, finely chopped
½ cup heavy cream	½ cup finely ground bread crumbs
3 Tbs of very good quality mayonnaise	1 tsp red pepper flakes
Juice and zest of 1 medium lemon	Salt and pepper to taste
2 cloves garlic, crushed, peeled and minced	½ cup balsamic vinegar reduced by half
5 black olives, finely chopped	

In a food processor, pulse the tuna, cream, mayonnaise, lemon zest, lemon juice, red pepper flakes, finely ground bread crumbs, and garlic. Add the black and green olives and give the processor a very quick pulse to evenly mix everything.

Place into a liberally-greased ramekin or loaf pan lined with plastic wrap. Refrigerate overnight. Invert and un-mold the loaf or ramekin onto a serving platter. Remove any plastic wrap stuck to the mousse. Serve with a drizzle of reduced balsamic vinegar sauce.

This is a rich and tasty mousse that goes well with crackers, Melba toast, or very thin toast points. It's easy to prepare in advance so you can spend some quality time with your guests during your party. You can also substitute lump crab meat instead of the tuna for a yummy crab mousse.

Basque Onion Soup

Serves 8

1 lb bone-in cooked beef (left over prime rib or rib eye steak is the best in this dish)	1 tsp salt
	2 cups beef stock (see page 38)
	3 cups chicken stock (see page 38)
2 Tbs butter	4 Tbs roux (see page 57)
1 Tbs olive oil	1 Tbs molasses
5 Large onions (about 1 lb)	2/3 cup dry red wine
3 garlic cloves, chopped	3 Tbs brandy
1 tsp sugar	

Heat the butter and oil in a heavy-bottomed, large skillet or pan. Add the onions, stir well, cover, and cook over very low heat, stirring occasionally for 15 minutes. Uncover the pan and increase the heat to medium. Stir in the garlic, sugar and 1 tsp salt. Cook, stirring frequently for about 30 - 40 minutes, or until the onions are a deep golden brown.

Meanwhile, in a stock pot bring the beef stock and chicken stock to a slow boil. Add the roux. Add the molasses. Cut cooked beef into small pieces, including all the fat, add to the stock. Add the bone to the stock pot as well.

Add the browned onion mixture to the stock pot. Deglaze the onion pan with the dry red wine scraping up all the tasty bits and pieces of onion left in the pan. Add brandy. Add this deglazed liquid from the onion pan to the soup pot. Cook for an additional 20 minutes, skimming any foam that comes to the top. Remove the beef bone. Serve hot.

Chef's notes - This soup is usually served as a single serving with melted Gruyere cheese on top and a side of French bread. Many French onion soups use a vegetable base with no meat at all. However, I like meat and this is the best way I know to use up left over prime rib, or the extra pieces of steak left over from dinner don't forget the doggy bags next time you go out for prime rib. Be sure to bring home the bones, not for your dog – for the soup pot!

Beef Stock
Makes 1 ½ quarts

3 lb meaty beef bones	5 celery ribs, chopped into large pieces, including the leafy tops
2 medium yellow onions, peeled and quartered	1 cup dry red wine
2 unpeeled carrots, cut into large pieces	Cold water

Preheat oven to 425 degrees.

Place beef bones into a lightly oiled baking pan. Cook for 15 minutes. Into the same baking pan, add the carrots and onions, bake for an additional 45 minutes, stirring occasionally to prevent vegetables from burning.

Transfer beef bones, meat scraps, and roasted vegetables to a large stock pot. Deglaze the roasting pan with the red wine making sure to scrape all the crusty bits and pieces from the bottom of the pan. Add this to the stock pot. Add enough cold water to cover everything, (approximately 6 cups). Bring to a rolling boil, reduce heat to low, and simmer for 2 hours. Skim any foam that may rise to the top, collect and discard.

Remove the vegetables and beef bones. Strain the liquid through a cheesecloth lined colander. Refrigerate overnight. Remove any fat that collects at the top of the broth and discard. Can be kept in the refrigerator for 1 week or in the freezer for up to 3 months. The beef broth will be in a gelatin-like state one cooled. It will melt into a liquid when heated.

Beef broth is something you need to know how to make; but feel free to use the store bought kind if that makes life easier.

Chicken Stock
Makes about 2 quarts

1 whole chicken, cut into parts	1 leek, trimmed and chopped into coarse pieces
2 peeled and coarsely chopped onions	Salt and pepper to taste
2 ribs celery chopped into one inch pieces	1 bouquet garni
1 large unpeeled carrot, cut into 3 or 4 pieces	¼ cup cooking oil
½ cup chopped fresh parsley	1 cup white wine
	2 quarts cold water

Except for the white wine, salt, and water, place all ingredients into a large stock pot and brown over medium heat in batches. As each batch is browned, set aside. Deglaze the pan with the white wine. Add everything back to the stock pot

and cover all with cold water. Bring to a gentle boil, skim and discard any foam that may collect. Reduce the heat to a slow simmer. Simmer partially covered for 4-6 hours, skimming occasionally. As the liquid reduces be aware the broth becomes more concentrated, hence saltier. Do not over salt or you will be sorry. Do not add any salt until the very end; you may not need any at all.

Pour the broth through a strainer lined with cheesecloth and refrigerate (usually overnight) until the fat rises to the surface and can be easily removed. After refrigeration and with the fat removed, you will find the chicken stock will be in a gelatin like state. Once it heats up it liquefies again.

Freeze some in ice cube trays, then place in a plastic freezer bag and you will always have a quick supply of tasty chicken stock.

Chef's notes – You can also get chicken broth from the drippings and water added when making Roasted Rosemary Chicken (see page 84). After the chicken and vegetables are removed, run the juice through a cheesecloth lined strainer and process the same way.

Occasionally the broth gets too salty because of too much reduction. The liquid is evaporating off as it reduces, the salts stays behind. If you get broth that's too salty, sometimes you can save it by adding a quartered raw potato to the broth and cooking for about 45 minutes. The potato will absorb salt. If it is still too salty, try adding more liquid, (i.e., wine or water or more stock) to dilute the saltiness. Remember to always taste your way through everything you cook. After you have reduced it – taste it. How salty is it? If it seems salty enough, don't add any more salt, even if the recipe calls for it.

I have added this basic stock recipe so you can make your own. But the kind you get at the store is perfectly fine to use and can make your cooking project easier if you don't have stock on hand.

Chilled Tomato Gazpacho Soup
Serves 6

1 onion, peeled and quartered	*1 6-oz can tomato paste*
1 red bell pepper, seeds removed	*3 14-oz cans chopped tomatoes and juices (or use 3 lbs fresh peeled and seeded tomatoes)*
1 tsp chopped garlic	
2 Tbs paprika	*1 cup chicken stock*
½ tsp cumin	*1 ½ cups ice water*
Pinch red pepper flakes	*1 ½ cups breadcrumbs*
1 tsp black pepper	*Garnish (see below)*
1 tsp balsamic vinegar (or any kind of vinegar)	

Except for the tomatoes, chicken stock, ice water, and breadcrumbs, place all ingredients into a food processor and process until a thick paste is created.

Into a large stockpot place one cup of chicken stock and reduce by half. Add all the chopped tomatoes including juices, the tomato paste, and the ice water. Add the processed paste to the soup mixture, add breadcrumbs and mix everything together well. Refrigerate for at least 2 hours, overnight is better. Serve chilled, garnished with a relish made from the following fresh raw vegetables:

- Seeded chopped cucumber
- Chopped fresh cilantro
- Chopped red bell pepper
- Chopped scallions
- Chopped avocado

A dollop of crème fraische or sour cream on top is a nice way to finish the garnish.

Chef's Notes – Gazpacho was originally a MRE (meal-ready-to-eat) for the Roman legions. Oil and bread were issued to each solider as their food ration and they would soak the bread in water, squeezing out the moisture leaving a paste and then they would mix it with the oil adding whatever protein and vegetables they could find along the way as they campaigned. It wasn't until the mid 1700's that it became associated with tomatoes when that vegetable was reintroduced from the Americas to Europe. Before then, it was a commonly held belief in Europe that tomatoes were toxic. In fact, the plates were made of lead and the acid in the tomatoes would cause the lead to leach into food – which poisoned people. So it was the lead plates, not the tomatoes themselves, that were toxic. Can you imagine Italy with no tomatoes?

Creamy Tomato Basil Soup
Serves 6

2 cups chicken or vegetable stock	1 tsp salt
1 qt whole milk	¼ cup sugar
3 lb peeled, seeded, and chopped tomatoes (or 3 14-oz cans chopped tomatoes, with juice)	1 Tbs dried basil
	Crème fraische (see page 63)
1 6-oz can tomato paste	

Place stock into soup pot over medium high heat and cook until the stock is reduced by half. Combine all the other ingredients except for basil into the soup pot. Bring to a slow boil. If milk separates, continue to boil until milk re-incorporates. Use an emersion blender to help emulsify the milk fat back into the soup. If it still looks a little like cottage cheese, don't worry about it, it still tastes great. Cook for about 45 minutes. Give it a stir and a taste. Add dried basil during last 15 minutes. Garnish with crème fraische.

Chef's notes - At the restaurant, this is the soup that everyone wants to take home. It is truly the best tomato soup you ever had. But I have to tell you this funny story about when my family came to have dinner one night. I served this soup and my brother started making a face and raking his finger across his throat as if to say, "I'm dying!" He mouthed the words "tooooo salty!" I ran to the soup pot and tasted the soup. He was right, it tasted like salt! Somehow salt was added in the place of the sugar – in that amount. Remember when I told you to always taste your way through what you are cooking. That is why. I was so embarrassed! Here I am trying to show off in front of my family and I really blow it big time. It's embarrassing to make that kind of really stupid mistake. My brother still razzes me about it. ALWAYS taste your way through what you cook.

Fish Stock
Makes 1 quart

2 fish heads, gills removed	½ cup chicken stock
3 Tbs olive oil	1 large bouquet garni with 5 pepper corns, 1 bay leaf, 2 Tbs dry thyme, and a large sprig of parsley,
2 large onions, finely chopped	
6 cloves crushed garlic	4 cups water
1 cup white wine	Salt and pepper to taste
2 lbs fish bones	

Put olive oil in heavy-bottomed stock pot over medium heat. Add onions and garlic and sauté till brown. Add wine to deglaze the pan and then add fish heads, fish bones, bouquet garni, chicken stock, and enough water to cover the fish. Cover and simmer for approximately 2 hours. Strain the liquid and discard the heads, bones, and veggies, and bouquet garni. Pour the strained liquid back into the stock pot and reduce by half. Add salt and pepper to taste.

You can refrigerate the stock for up to one week or freeze for up to 3 months. Don't forget to label and date it as it will look just like chicken stock.

Chef's notes - Whenever I make fish stock, I always find myself singing the comedy song "fish heads, fish heads, yummy, yummy fish heads". Do you remember that song? No? Oh well, I'm old. Anyway, fish heads are one of the main ingredients in fish stock. Talk to your local fish monger, or butcher, or meat guy or gal at the market meat counter, about saving you fish bones and heads a few days before you want to make the stock. Just make sure you are using fish heads and bones that are still considered "fresh". Fish stock is usually not available at your local market so this is one you will probably need to make yourself.

Mirepoix Soup
Serves 4

3 Tbs butter	¼ cup sugar
1 cup chopped carrots	2 cups chicken or vegetable stock
1 cup chopped celery	Salt and pepper to taste
1 cup chopped onions	Crème fraische (see page 63)
1 qt whole milk	

In a heavy skillet, melt butter and cook carrots first. They are a little tougher and take a little longer to cook. Cover and let them steam for a few minutes. When they are fork tender, add the celery and onions and continue cooking until the onions are translucent. Take sautéed carrots, celery, and onions (aka mirepoix) and any juices from the pan, place into a food processor and process until a thick paste or puree is created. You may need to add a little stock to the food processor to get the vegetables to blend well and puree. You don't want any chunky pieces of carrots, celery, or onions.

In a stock pot, reduce 2 cups of stock by half. Add puree mixture and add remaining ingredients (except for crème fraische), and cook for 45 minute, Stirring occasionally. Taste and add salt and pepper as needed.

Garnish with a dollop of crème fraische.

Pumpkin Soup

Serves 6

2 lbs pumpkin or butternut squash (or one large 29-oz can whole pumpkin)	1 tsp salt
	¼ cup sugar
2 cups chicken stock or vegetable stock	crème fraische (see page 63)
1 qt whole milk	

Preheat oven to 350 degrees.

Cut squash into big chunks and place on baking sheet pan, rind side up. Bake in oven for 1 hour or until fork tender. Remove from oven and let cool. Remove seeds and pith. Remove cooked pumpkin or winter squash flesh from rind and place in food processor. Add ½ cup of milk and process until a smooth paste is made, or use prepared canned pumpkin.

In soup pot cook 2 cups of stock until reduced by half. Add remaining milk and all the other ingredients except crème fraische. Add squash puree and simmer over medium low heat for 45 minutes. Garnish with a dollop of crème fraische on each serving.

Rabbit Stew

Serves 6 to 8

2 - 3 lb rabbit meat	¼ tsp tarragon
3 cloves garlic, crushed and chopped	1 Tbs coarse ground pepper
1 large white or yellow onion, chopped	1 tsp salt
2 carrots, chopped	5 cups water (enough to cover rabbit meat)
2 ribs celery, chopped	
2 whole dried bay leaves	2 Tbs butter
½ tsp dried thyme	3 - 5 Tbs roux (see page 57)

Put half of the vegetables and all of the spices into a large stock pot. Add the rabbit pieces, bones and all. Heat over medium high heat until the water starts to boil. Reduce heat to medium and simmer for about 2 hours. You can test for doneness by taking some metal tongs and see if the meat easily falls away from the bone. Remove the rabbit and bones from the pot and de-bone the rabbit pieces. Put the bones back into the broth in the pot. Refrigerate the cooked rabbit.

Simmer the broth for another 2 hours, leave the lid on the pot, occasionally skimming and discarding any foam that may collect. Once it's done simmering, strain the broth through a colander lined with cheese cloth and set the clear broth aside. Discard the stewed vegetables.

Take the rabbit meat out of the refrigerator and allow to come to room temperature. In the meantime, add the butter to a heavy bottomed pan, and add the other half of the veggies. Add 1 more clove of crushed garlic, garlic is our friend. Cook until the vegetables are al dente. Add 3 cups of the strained rabbit broth. Using a wooden spoon, deglaze the pan with the added broth.

Add approximately 3 tablespoons of roux to the broth. Cook for a few minutes on medium high heat. Test the broth for thickness. If you want it thicker, add more roux until you get the consistency you like. After all, it's your stew - have it your way. Now add back the pieces of rabbit meat and simmer until meat is hot. Serve with crusty bread for dipping.

Chef's notes – An old vaudeville comedian, W.C. Fields, was once quoted as saying "I love children, as long as they are properly prepared." I feel the same away about rabbit; when they are properly prepared they are fabulous. Just don't think about how cute and cuddly they can be. I would venture to bet the kids will even like this dish as long as you don't call it Bunny Stew. Probably not the best choice at Easter time either.

Vegetable Stock
Makes 1 ½ quarts

¼ cup cooking oil	3 lbs tomatoes, skinned and seeded (or 3 14-oz cans of chopped tomatoes including the juices)
3 large potatoes, quartered, skins on	
3 yellow onions, peeled and quartered	1 tsp salt
3 unpeeled carrots, cut into large pieces	1 tsp pepper
1 stalk celery, chopped coarsely including the leafy tops	½ cup dry red or white wine
10 cloves garlic, crushed and peeled	Cold water to cover the vegetables

Place all the ingredients, except wine and water, into a heavy - bottomed stock pot. Brown in batches, set aside. When everything is browned, deglaze the pan with ½ cup dry red or white wine. Add everything back into the stock pot and cover with cold water (approximately 6 cups). Simmer for two hours. Strain liquid through a colander lined with cheese cloth. Discard veggies. Return vegetable stock back to the stock pot and reduce by half. Test for flavor as you reduce the liquid. Too much reduction will result in a stock that has a bitter flavor.

Chef's notes – You can reduce any liquid to make a more intensely flavored liquid, including stock. If you are looking to save calories, do what those fru fru health spa's do – substitute reduced stock for butter or cooking oil to bring down the total fat content for any dish without losing flavor.

House Vinaigrette

Makes about 2 cups

1 cup good quality olive oil	1 tsp salt
½ cup vinegar (I like apple)	1 tsp coarse ground pepper
1 Tbs balsamic vinegar	1 tsp granulated garlic
2 Tbs honey	1 sprig fresh rosemary
1 tsp sweet dry basil	1 dried bay leaf
1 tsp tarragon	

Place all ingredients, accept the fresh rosemary and dried bay leaf, into a jar or bowl with high sides. Use an emersion blender and emulsify all the ingredients into a dressing. When well blended, add the fresh rosemary sprig and bay leaf into the dressing and put it all in a jar with a lid. Refrigerate for about 1 hour before using. If need be, shake well before serving. Don't serve the rosemary sprig or the bay leaf, but leave them in the jar as they will continue to add flavor.

California San Miguel Salad

Serves 6

1 bag baby lettuces spring mix	2 Tbs bleu cheese crumbles
5 leaves romaine lettuce, cut into bite-sized pieces	1 firm but ripe Anjou or Asian pear, cut into slices
½ cup spiced walnuts or pecans	1 ripe avocado (optional), cut into slices
1 cup simple syrup	
1 Tbs sugar	½ cup dried sweetened cranberries, or fresh raspberries
1 tsp cinnamon	3 Tbs house vinaigrette dressing (see page 47)
1 lime	

Preheat oven to 400 degrees.

Make spiced nuts by placing nuts on cookie sheet lined with parchment paper. Mix the sugar and cinnamon and have ready to sprinkle onto the nuts. Make the simple syrup by melting ½ cup of sugar and ½ cup water in the microwave. Put the syrup into a spray bottle and lightly spray the nuts with the sugary mixture. While the nuts are still wet from the sugar-spray, sprinkle with the sugar and cinnamon mixture. Immediately place into a preheated 400 degrees oven for about 10 to 15 minutes. (I always make a whole bunch of them at one time and keep in the freezer for use later on. They freeze well and last a long time.) Let cool before using.

Take the lime and squeeze the juice into a small bowl. Core and slice the pear into several thin slices and place the pear slices into the lime juice. This is done so the pear slices don't turn brown (some people peel the pear, but I like the color of the skin against the white fruit. It looks nice in the salad. If you use an Asian pear, peel that one, as the skin is tough.) Save the lime juice so you can repeat the process with a peeled and sliced avocado. The citric acid keeps fragile fruits from oxidizing too quickly and turning brown.

Place sliced pears into the salad greens. Add the sliced avocado. Add the sweetened dried cranberries or fresh raspberries, bleu cheese crumbles. Toss with approx 3 Tbs of the house vinaigrette along with the lime zest.

Chef's notes - I always recommend making the salad at the very last minute so it is at its freshest. If you are making salad for a big gathering, you can prepare the romaine a day ahead of time. Instead of cutting the lettuce with a knife, pull off bite- sized pieces of the romaine away from the rib in the middle. Discard the rib. The rib part is what bruises and turns brown when you hold it over night. When we have catering jobs and I know that my time is very limited, I always prepare the lettuce this way and refrigerate it, loosely covered. It will remain crisp, fresh, and un-bruised until the next day. Add all the other ingredients just before serving.

Croutons

Makes 2 cups

2 cups day old bread, cubed	Salt
Spray oil	1 Tbs granulated garlic

Preheat oven to 400 degrees.

Place cubed bread in one layer on baking sheet. Spray generously with oil. (Note that you don't need to buy spray oil, simply put cooking oil in a spray bottle, and viola!) Sprinkle with salt and granulated garlic. Place in heated oven for about 10 - 15 minutes. They will turn golden brown when done. Remove from oven and store in a container that is NOT air tight - they need to breathe. Use on salads or on anything that needs a little crispy boost.

You can also make croutons by taking bread cubes and deep frying them. I actually like them that way best - but it takes a little more time and you have to stand there and watch them. When browned, remove from the frying oil and place in a bowl and toss with salt.

You can add different dried spices and herbs for unique flavored croutons. Try granulated garlic, basil, tarragon, onion flakes- even parmesan cheese -see which one becomes your favorite.

Chef's notes - Stop buying those tasteless cardboard croutons you get at the grocery store. Same goes for stuffing mixtures. Make your own! Any kind of bread works. After cooking, they keep for a week. You can use them all week long in salads or anything else you want to add a crunchy texture too.

Caprese Salad
Serves 4

3 large heirloom tomatoes (different colors if you can get them) *Fresh basil* *½ lb sliced mozzarella cheese*	*1 cup balsamic vinegar* *½ cup extra virgin olive oil* *Salt and pepper to taste*

Place balsamic vinegar in a small sauce pan over medium heat. Cook until the liquid is reduced by half. The vinegar will begin to thicken and end up quite syrupy.

Cut tomatoes into slices cut, so you end up with round slices of tomato. De-stem all the basil. On a platter, arrange the sliced tomato, basil, and cheese, one after the other in a repeated pattern down the whole plate. You may have to cut the cheese so that is approximately the same size as the tomatoes. You may end up with two rows depending on how big the tomatoes are. When so arranged, drizzle with reduced balsamic vinegar and a very good, flavorful olive oil. Sprinkle with salt and pepper to taste.

You can make these on a large platter to be used on a buffet table or around a casual dinner table - or you can dress it up and serve it on individual plates decorating the plates with the balsamic vinegar syrup.

Chef's notes - I like to make this mid-summer when the tomatoes are sweet and plentiful and the basil is abundant. It's hard to make in the winter time because the ingredients just aren't available. A word to the wise, hot house tomatoes just don't cut it.

Cabbage Lime Cilantro Slaw
Serves 6

1 large head green cabbage	*¾ cup mayonnaise*
1 bunch fresh cilantro	*1 Tbs sugar*
4 limes	

Cut cabbage into very thin strips, cutting out, and discarding the tough inner core. Set cut cabbage aside in large mixing bowl.

Cut most of stems off the cilantro and put the leafy part into the food processor, discarding the stems. (Or you can save the stem for use if you are going to be making a bouquet garni any time soon.) Add zest from two of the limes into the food processor with the cilantro. Be careful not to zest off the bitter white pith between the fruit and rind. After zesting, cut all four limes in half and squeeze the juice into the food processor with the other ingredients. Add the mayonnaise and sugar and process the mixture for about 1 minute. You want the cilantro to be finely chopped when finished. Pour this dressing onto the cut cabbage, mix well, chill for about an hour and serve cold.

Chef's notes - Instead of zesting and squeezing limes, you can use a small can of frozen limeade juice and leave out the sugar. Just put everything in the food processor and give it all a wiz. Easy peasy. We like to serve this at the restaurant under some of the meat dishes we serve as Tapas, as a tasty side dish. It makes a very nice presentation contrasting its pale green color against something like pork brochettes in a red sauce. It is also a killer served with any kind of meat in tacos. We even serve it as a standalone dish, as a palate cleanser between courses.

Basque Bread

Makes 3 loaves

Starter

¼ cup sugar	¼ cup warm water (85 -100 degrees)
2 Tbs yeast	

Bread

5 cups flour	¼ cup sugar
2 cups warm water (85 – 100 degrees)	1 Tbs salt
2 Tbs cooking oil	¼ cup basil

Preheat oven to 375 degrees.

Place *Starter* ingredients in a bowl and mix thoroughly. Set aside to let double in size – this should take about 20 minutes. If the water is over 100 degrees the yeast may die.

While the *Starter* is doing its magic yeast thing, place the *Bread* ingredients into a mixer with a dough hook. The mixing bowl should be about three times the size of the ingredients.

When the *Starter* has doubled, add it to the *Bread* ingredients in the mixing bowl. Make sure the yeast mixture has in fact doubled in size before mixing it into the *Bread* ingredients.

If the yeast hasn't *proofed*, term used to let you know the yeast has indeed proven that it is still alive, try again. Make sure the water is not too hot (over 100 degrees) – water that is too hot will kill the yeast. Use an instant read thermometer to make sure you are right at 85-100 degrees. If it still doesn't double, you may need new yeast. If you are using yeast that you found in the back of the spice rack and probably purchased at Thanksgiving 2 years ago, it's too old!

Mix the dough for about 12 minutes with the dough hook or for about 10 minutes by hand. You need to mix it for this long to develop the gluten. Gluten makes for great bread. If you are using the dough hook, check the bread dough. If it is pulling away from the sides of the bowl and climbing a little bit up the dough hook, it is the right texture. If it is still juicy and looking very sticky, add more flour ½ a cup at a time until the bread dough is a smooth, springy texture. It should be pulling cleanly away from the mixing bowl as it is kneaded by the dough hook.

If you are mixing the dough by hand, knead the dough by turning it out onto a floured surface. For best results, press with the heels of your hand. Press the dough down and out and then fold back onto and into itself and press down again and fold back over again. Repeat this process over and over for about 10 minutes. If the dough wants to stick to your hands and seems too wet and sticky add more flour ½ a cup at a time, until the dough stops sticking to your hands. Sometimes you can simply rub your hands with some cooking oil to keep the dough from sticking to your hands. However, if it still won't let go and begins to build upon itself on your hands as you knead, it is still too wet. Add some flour.

Set the kneaded dough into a bowl that you have sprayed lightly with cooking oil, cover with a moist dish towel (or plastic wrap) and let sit in a warm area away from drafts. If you used the mixer to mix your dough, you can leave it in that same bowl. Let double in size, about 45 minutes. If it has not doubled in that time, move to a warmer area and wait for it to double - don't get impatient, sometimes it takes as long as 2 or 3 hours for dough to rise.

You can tell when the dough has risen enough when a slightly moistened finger will leave a dent that doesn't spring back.

When it has doubled, punch down the dough, knocking much of the air out of it. Cut into three balls of dough, about 1 lb each. Working the dough in your hands, form a football shaped loaf stretching the top side of the dough down and under itself, tucking and working it to the under-side. Once it is shaped, place each football shaped dough ball into its own loaf pan, cover with moistened dish towels, and let rise again.

If you don't have loaf pans, not to worry: make boles - a round loaf. Follow the same instructions as above, except make 3 round loaves. Divide the dough into three balls. Pull down against the side of each dough ball with your left hand and gently pushing up with the right hand so the dough rotates through your hands in a counterclockwise motion, stretching, rotating, and tucking the dough until you have a nice rounded dome shaped loaf. Place on a cookie sheet, cover, and let rise to double its size.

After the loaves (either the ones in the bread pans or the boles) have risen, score each loaf with a very shape knife about 4 times, cutting across the loaf ¼ to ½ inch deep. This allows steam to escape while baking, otherwise it explodes and you have a messy loaf of bread that doesn't cook well. Do not forget to score it!

Cook in preheated 375 degree oven. Once it is in the oven, take a spray bottle filled with salted water and spray the inside of the oven making sure each loaf gets misted in the process. This will give you a crusty, slightly salted crust. Spray the salt water again into the oven at the 15 minute mark. Continue to bake for about 30 - 45 minutes. Check at 30 minutes with an instant read thermometer. It should be 180 degrees. If it is not that temperature internally, but the tops are already browned, cover loaves loosely with foil and continue cooking. Just because the crust looks brown doesn't mean the middle is cooked. If you don't reach 180 degrees internally, the inside will be gooey and undercooked. Once the internal temperature reaches 180 – 200 degrees, remove from oven and be prepared to eat an entire loaf – it'll be that good.

Chef's notes - Bread is alive, it's alive! Every time you make it, you have to check the dough as it kneads. Even though you use exactly the same ingredients, the weather affects it. The humidity in the air affects it. If it is too dry, it affects it. If it is going to storm and the barometric pressure rises or lowers, it affects. If it is cold outside; you need to find a warmer place to let it rise. Yes indeed, bread has a life of its own. But it is very satisfying to make when it turns out well. I don't know how to explain it – it's one of those things you have to experience to understand.

Cheesy Basque Biscuits
Makes 24 biscuits

2 ½ cups flour	3 Tbs grated Swiss cheese
1/3 cup non-fat powdered milk	3 Tbs grated mozzarella or jack cheese
1 Tbs baking powder	8 Tbs chilled butter, cut into pieces
Pinch of salt	1 cup cold water
3 Tbs grated cheddar cheese	Spray oil

Preheat oven to 425 degrees.

Place all the dry ingredients into the bowl of a food processor with the "S" steel blade. Pulse to mix well. Open top of food processor and add all three chees-

es. Close it up and pulse a few more times until everything is cut into small pieces. Turn machine onto medium speed and add, all at once, the cold water through the opening at the top of the operating food processor.

Keep an eye on it. The moment it begins to incorporate, turn it off. It will be a tad chunky. Take a 24 piece muffin tin and spray with a fine mist of spray oil. Spoon the batter into each cup a little more than half full.

Bake in preheated 425 degree oven for about 10 to 15 minutes, or until they are lightly golden. Insert a tooth pick into the center- when the biscuits are done, it should come out clean. Remove from muffin tins ASAP and allow to air dry for a few minutes. Serve warm.

Nina's Parmesan Rolls
Makes 16 rolls

2 Packages store bought refrigerated uncooked crescent rolls in the round container.	*½ cup grated parmesan cheese* *½ stick salted butter, melted*

Preheat oven to 375 degrees.

Line a baking sheet with parchment paper. Place rolls on to paper and brush liberally with melted butter. Sprinkle each roll with parmesan cheese and place in preheated oven until golden brown. This is a wonderful easy and tasty side dish, thanks Nina.

Pastry Dough
Makes two 9" pie crusts, one large empanada, or approximately 8 small individual empanadas.

2 ½ cups flour	*1 tsp white vinegar*
3 Tbs chilled butter, cut into pieces	*Pinch of salt*
2 Tbs chilled vegetable shortening, cut into pieces	*1/3 cup icy water* *Egg wash*

Place flour, butter and shortening pieces into food processor with the "S" steel blade attached. Pulse several times until the butter and shortening is well cut into the flour. About 4 or 5 pulses. Add the vinegar and salt. With the processor running at a medium speed, gradually add the ice water through the opening in the top of the food processor. Watch the dough as you add water. You may not need all the water. When the dough just begins to ball up, stop the food processor. Do not over process or the pastry will be tough. Open the lid and see if the dough will hold together when you squeeze it. If you find that it will not stick together enough to be able to roll out, add a little bit more ice water and process again. Add a little at a time, too much will make it too sticky. Once again, be careful not to over process

dough or you will end up with a tough crust. Once it just sticks together when squeezed, remove from the processor and form into two evenly-sized balls. Place in a mixing bowl and cover with plastic wrap and refrigerate at least ½ hour. You want the butter and shortening to be well chilled in the mixture so you can roll it out and not tear it.

When ready to line your pie pan or make empanadas, evenly roll each dough ball out onto floured surface, about ¼" thick, and cut to desired size. For individual empanadas, we use the open end of a large water glass to cut them. Dip the glass into a bit of flour first.

For an extra golden crust, when dough has been arranged over pie filling, or folded into an empanada, brush with egg wash just before cooking. Also, use the egg wash to get the empanada top to stick to its bottom half, use the egg wash like a glue to get pastry to stick to itself.

Some recipes require the bottom pastry be cooked first. Cut and place pie dough in bottom of pan, line top with foil, weigh down with dried beans, or pastry weights, and cook for 8 - 10 minutes.

Chef's notes – We use this pie dough recipe for both sweet and savory dishes. From fruit pies to empanadas, this flakey dough works well.

Geez, where do you start with sauces? Sauces can take you to new heights as a cook because they are like the frosting on cake. The cake has to be there and be tasty, but we all know it's the frosting that makes or breaks it. Sauce is the same way. If you can master sauces you can master serving fabulous food. The most important thing about sauces is ROUX! (Pronounced "roo"). You will find this magical ingredient called out in many recipes in this book. Most cookbooks tell you to add 2 Tbs of flour to 2 Tbs butter or fat as you cook, making the thickener when you make the dish. But you can end up with lumps that won't go away, a dish that still tastes like flour, and no ability to additionally thicken your sauces. If you are unhappy with the texture and viscosity of the sauces you have made in the past, learn to make roux. Make more than you need and keep it on hand.

Roux is magic. Don't let the French name or spelling intimidate you. It is considered the "mother" for classical sauces. We usually make roux with equal parts of butter and flour, but any fat will work.

We have put the recipe for Roux first in the sauce chapter because many of the subsequent recipes call for it. If you learn nothing else from this book, learn this part. It will turn you into the kind of cook you always wanted to be.

Roux
Makes about 1 ½ cups

1 lb butter	3 cups flour

Melt butter on stove top in a heavy skillet, add flour slowly, a cup at a time, stirring continuously. With butter and flour completely combined, let it cook stirring occasionally. It will take on the consistently of cooked oatmeal. As it cooks and begins to brown it will begin to smell of roasted nuts. Be aware that the darker the roux becomes the less it will thicken, but the flavor is enhanced the darker it gets. The lighter colored roux will thicken sauces, soups, and gravies the most, but a roux cooked to the color of mahogany will add a lot of flavor but less thickening to those same sauces, soups, and gravies.

You want to cook the fat and flour long enough so that it smells like nuts and turns at least a light golden color.

Don't use it before that happens or you will taste the flour in your soup or sauce.

When making turkey gravy, use the fat from the cooked turkey with an equal amount of flour and make a roux from that. Just be sure it cooks long enough so

the flour no longer has that pasty taste. Once the roux is cooked and creamy, you can add it to the hot stock and drippings. Whisk continuously while adding roux to make lump free, absolutely delicious turkey gravy. This method will work with any fat and flour based sauce, soup, or gravy. Use with any fat and pan drippings from meats, fish, chicken, and vegetables to create sauce. Usually, I remove the food from the pan, leaving any fat and drippings in the pan, deglaze the pan with a little wine, and add roux. Voila – Sauce!

Biscuits and gravy? Sausage fat mixed with equal parts flour, cooked until the flour begins to turn golden, add a cup or so of milk, some of the crumbled sausage, and cook until gravy is the right consistency. Ladle over biscuits!

A plain sautéed chicken breast can become gourmet fare by removing the chicken breast from the pan, set aside and keep warm and then deglaze the pan with a little white wine, add a few chopped mushrooms, a little roux and ta daa - chicken for company!.

This recipe will make a lot of roux. Make a bunch and have it on hand. Once cooked, place onto parchment paper in a thin layer and refrigerate and let it harden into a bark. You can then break this bark into pieces and store in a plastic zip lock bag so you always have roux available whenever you are cooking. Another way to keep roux handy is to fill an ice cube tray with the hot roux mixture and refrigerate or freeze. This will give you a more controlled portion.

Personally, I just add roux bark until I get the consistency I want for a particular sauce or gravy. The more roux added the thicker the sauce will be. Easy peasy. I promise you many oooohs and ahhhs when you come to the table with a killer sauce.

When you are thickening a sauce with roux, you have to cook it a minute or two before it will begin to thicken. Add a little to start, and keep adding and cooking until you get the desired consistency.

Almond Paste
Makes 2 cups

1 lb almonds	6 Tbs good honey
5 Tbs almond extract (buy the best you can find)	8 egg whites

Blanch the almonds and remove the skins by rubbing with your fingers (or buy them already blanched). Pulse the almonds in a food processor until they are very fine. Add the honey, almond extract, and egg whites and pulse until all the ingredients are thoroughly mixed together forming a paste. Refrigerate in a covered container.

Chef's notes - There is an old Basque proverb that goes something like this, "Women, gold, dogs, and sheep should only be chosen in daylight and almond paste should only be eaten when in love." If that is the case, then the Basque people must always be in love because they use almond paste in a myriad of dishes from main courses to desserts. Anytime is a good time to be in love. Make almond paste.

Warning!! Never put your finger down the throat of an operating food processor just to get that last ingredient to go in. It's not worth it! Your next stop will be the emergency room.

Ancho Chili Sauce
Makes 2 cups

12 dried Ancho chilies	½ tsp brown sugar
3 Tbs olive oil	1 tsp chocolate sauce
2 medium yellow onions, chopped	2 Tbs canned Chipotle peppers, chopped
3 cloves garlic crushed and finely chopped	½ cup heavy cream
1 14-oz can chopped tomatoes with juice	Salt and pepper to taste

Clean the Ancho chilies under cold water being careful to remove and discard the seeds and stems. Place the chilies in a bowl of hot water for at least one hour, re-hydrating them, until they are soft and tender. Drain and dry them with paper towels. Heat the oil in a heavy skillet and add the onion and garlic. Cook until browned and add the Ancho chilies, chopped tomatoes and juice, sugar, and chocolate sauce. Cook for approximately 20 minutes. Add the heavy cream. With an emersion blender, wiz everything together in the pan. Slowly add the chipotle peppers until you find the preferred level of heat.

This sauce will add a little zing to your creations when served on the side. It can be used as an ingredient as well, but we usually make it up as a dipping sauce for beef, lamb, or chicken.

Balsamic Vinegar Sauce
Makes 1 cup

2 cups balsamic vinegar	*2 Tbs honey*
Zest and juice of 1 lemon	*1 Tbs chocolate syrup*

Heat the balsamic vinegar, lemon juice, zest and honey over very low heat. Cook until the liquid has been reduced by at least half. The leftover liquid should smell sweet and look like very thin hot fudge. Add the chocolate sauce and serve over a number of different savory dishes. But what they hey, I have a chef friend who serves it over ice cream with fresh fruit! Be brave, be creative.

Chef's notes - You can use lower quality balsamic vinegar for this recipe because we are going to reduce the vinegar by at least half. Heat changes wine and vinegar, whether you use the expensive kind or the less expensive vinegar it won't make a bit of difference.

Basic Spanish Tomato Sauce
Makes 4 cups

2 Tbs olive oil	*1 large red bell pepper, coarsely chopped*
1 large white or yellow onion, coarsely chopped	*1 14-oz can chopped tomatoes, with juice*
1 rib celery, coarsely chopped	*Pinch of basil, thyme, coarse ground pepper, red pepper flakes*
2 cloves garlic, crushed, peeled, and chopped	
2 Tbs dried parsley	

In heavy skillet or heavy-bottomed pot, heat olive oil over medium high heat. Add onions, celery and garlic, lower heat and cook a few minutes more, until onions are almost browned. Add bell pepper and tomato; cook until bell pepper is tender. Using an emersion blender, wiz everything together. If you do not have an emersion blender, transfer all into food processor and process until smooth. Use this sauce in stews, or for brazing pork or beef brochettes, or over pasta.

Brown Butter Sauce
Makes ½ cup

1/2 lb unsalted butter (2 sticks)	

Place the butter in a light skillet. Don't use a heavy skillet because it will retain too much heat and will burn the butter, rather than just browning it. Cook the butter until it starts to take on a rich dark hue, but before it reaches its smoke point. Stop and immediately remove the butter to a cold pan. The difference between brown butter and burnt butter happens in a blink of an eye, so watch it. If it burns, don't even try to save it. Throw it away and try again.

Use this browned butter as a basting butter after you have cooked whatever kind of meat you are preparing, this adds a richness of flavor that only butter can, while allowing you to cook in other mediums, such as oil or broth. Add this sauce at the very end. It gives you a great buttery flavor without cooking, and usually burning, in butter. Brown Butter is a wonderful arrow to have in your quiver of culinary delights. Wow, I should be a poet.

Cilantro Lime Sauce

There are two ways to prepare this sauce, the easy way and the hard way. Let's start with the hard way for you purists out there.

The "Hard" Way
Makes 1 ¼ cups

1 cup olive oil	2 Tbs honey
4 whole limes	1 tsp salt
1 cup fresh cilantro	

Place the oil, the zest of 2 limes, and the juice from all four limes in a food processor. Add cilantro, salt, and honey. Process for 1 minute or until the cilantro is finely chopped and everything is well blended. Set aside for flavors to meld and store in refrigerator until needed.

The "Easy" Way
Makes 3 cups

1 cup olive oil	1 cup fresh cilantro
1 small frozen can of limeade	1 tsp salt

Put everything in a food processor. Wiz it up. That was easy!

Chef's notes - You will love this sauce. It is tasty and a beautiful color. We use this sauce on all kinds of things from fish cakes to fried cheese. It's also good on tacos. Try it on fruit salad. It has great flavor and color. Put it in a squeeze bottle and embellish (nap) plates and food.

Citrus Dip
Makes 1 cup

1 lemon, zest and juice	2 cloves fresh garlic, crushed, peeled, and minced
1 orange, zest and juice	1 Tbs honey
1 lime, zest and juice	Salt and pepper to taste
½ cup extra virgin olive oil	

Zest each of the citrus fruits. Then cut each in half and squeeze out the juices into a mixing bowl with the zest and other ingredients. Whisk all the ingredients until well incorporated.

You can ladle this sauce over cooked fish, chicken, or veggies. You can also place a small amount of sauce in individual sized ramekins for each person and they can dip their food into it. I always make a lot of this sauce- there is never any left.

Chef's notes - The real intense flavors of citrus fruits are contained in the oils of the rind. The best way to get to this "zest" is with a handy dandy micro planer. Be careful to zest away only the rind, the white part between the skin of the fruit and actual fruit is bitter - don't use that part. This dip/sauce has a myriad of layered flavors and is great for fish, chicken, and veggies.

Clarified Butter

1 lb salted butter	

Heat butter until totally melted. Simmer slowly so impurities and salts will settle out of the butter. Gently skim from the top any foam that may collect. Strain remaining butter through a sieve lined with cheese cloth. This will remove the rest of the solids leaving you with a clear, yummy, delicious butter.

This butter oil will have a much higher smoke point than normal butter, so you can cook at much higher temperatures. By using clarified butter, you get all the good flavor of butter without the risk of burning what you are cooking. When you go to restaurants where the chef is making omelets to order, look and see that he almost always uses clarified butter in the omelet pan - no burning, no sticking. Beautiful.

Crème Fraische
Makes 2 cups

2 cups cream or whole milk	4 Tbs cultured buttermilk

Place these two ingredients into a non metallic container and cover with plastic wrap. Take a toothpick and pierce the plastic wrap numerous times. Leave out on the counter overnight. In the morning, replace pierced plastic wrap with another piece of plastic wrap (not pierced) and refrigerate.

Homemade crème fraische will last about 1 week in the refrigerator. You can buy it already made, but it is a little pricey. It's so easy and inexpensive to make, make it yourself and feel free to use as much as you want. It is a fabulous tangy garnish on vegetables, and creamy soups, or as a base for dips. Use it in place of sour cream or yogurt in your other favorite recipes.

Diablo Sauce
Makes about 1½ cup

1 small can of chipotle peppers	1 lemon, zest and juice
2 Tbs chopped garlic	1 tsp salt
1 cup mayonnaise	

Place all the ingredients into a food processor and pulse till they are all incorporated. This is a wonderful, easy way to spice up a lot of dishes and it is yummy.

Dry Rub
Makes about 4 cups

2 cups brown sugar	1 Tbs granulated garlic
1 cup chili powder	1 Tbs coarse ground pepper
1 cup Kosher salt	1 Tbs Old Bay Spice
1 Tbs onion powder	

Mix all ingredients together, making a spice mixture. When ready to use, rub spices all over meat to flavor and tenderize. Refrigerate and let sit. Overnight is best, but at least 2 hours is required. The salt will pull liquid out of the meat and create a wonderful rich marinade.

Horseradish sauce
Makes about ½ cup

1 piece of horseradish root about as big as your thumb	*1 tsp honey*
¼ tsp salt	*A tiny dash of paprika*
2 Tbs sugar	*A tiny dash of lemon zest, less is better*
½ cup heavy cream	

Peel the horseradish root and grate. Mix everything else into it and have a taste. If your eyes tear up as if you had just seen the final scene in just about any "tear jerker" movie, you did it right. This sauce is great on beef and lamb.

Marinated Artichoke Hearts, Pesto, and Mushroom Sauce
Makes about 1 ¾ cups

1 cup sliced mushrooms	*2 Tbs oil from artichoke marinade*
2 Tbs butter	*¼ cup pesto sauce (see page 65)*
½ cup artichoke hearts, marinated in oil	*¼ cup mayonnaise*

Cook sliced mushrooms in the butter over medium heat until just beginning to brown. Place mushroom and melted butter into food processor. Add marinated artichoke hearts, oil, pesto, and mayonnaise. Process for about 1 minute or until a smooth sauce is created.

We like to serve this at room temperature as a topping for our albacore fish cakes (see page 21). It is also great heated up a little in the microwave and served on pork chops, pasta noodles, or on a boneless, skinless chicken breast. It really adds a lot of flavor to anything that needs a little extra zip.

Mint Sauce
Makes 2 ½ cups

1 cup olive oil	*¼ cup brown sugar*
¼ cup balsamic vinegar	*12 garlic cloves crushed, peeled, and minced*
¾ cup apple cider vinegar	*¼ tsp coarse ground pepper*
¾ cup fresh mint, chopped	*Salt to taste*
1 Tbs fresh rosemary chopped, stems removed	*2 Tbs fresh thyme, chopped*
¼ cup white sugar	

In a small sauce pan combine oil, vinegars, sugars, salt and pepper and bring to a boil. Add mint, rosemary, and garlic and refrigerate.

This is a wonderful easy sauce for lamb and will keep a long time in the refrigerator. It can be used as a marinade and can be served hot or cold or as a dipping sauce.

Pesto Sauce
Makes about 1½ cups

2 cups fresh basil	*½ cup olive oil*
1 tsp salt	*2/3 cup pine nuts*
1 lemon, zest and juice	*2 Tbs chopped garlic*
1 cup grated parmesan cheese	

Place all ingredients into a food processor and pulse until they are all incorporated. Make a ton of this sauce in the summertime when fresh basil is abundant. Freeze it in small portions for use all year. When you are making this sauce the whole kitchen will smell delicious. Use on its own as a sauce or as an ingredient in other recipes. We love it by itself on pasta, or throw some chicken in with it. Try it on pizza with jalapenos and sausage with a white sauce. Or use it as an ingredient like in the Marinated Artichoke Hearts, Pesto, and Mushroom Sauce.

Reduced Merlot Sauce
Makes about 1½ cups

1 cup beef stock	*½ cup drippings from meat being served*
2 cups merlot wine (or any hearty dry red you have on hand)	*2 Tbs roux (see page 57)*
1 Tbs honey	

Over medium high heat, cook 1 cup of beef stock and 2 cups of red wine until reduced by half. Add honey and pan drippings, mix well. Add roux. Cook until desired thickness. If too thin, add more roux, if too thick add more wine. You don't want this sauce too thick. The sauce should be somewhat thin so as to enhance the flavor of the meat, not mask it.

Chef's notes - We are of the opinion that you drink the good wine, and you cook with the stuff you really don't want to drink. I know, I know, on TV every celebrity chef out there says to use the best wine for sauces that you can afford. Well, I'm sorry, being a wine guy *and* a food guy - I say "bunk!" Drink the good stuff, cook with the not so good stuff. Also, if you have ½ a bottle of wine left over from two nights ago - cook with that wine. It's oxidized. I promise it won't taste like it did the day you opened it. However, you can certainly use it for cooking with no problem! I always die when I see a celebrity chef taking a perfectly good bottle of expensive wine and pour it into a sauce or soup or use as a cooking liquid for braising or poaching... the minute the wine is exposed to such extreme heat, it is no longer the magical elixir it once was in the bottle. It's called chemistry - it changes when it gets hot. However, if you are cooking, and drinking wine while you do so, you can always add some of what you are drinking if you want to. I'm too cheap to cook with the really good wine; I only want to drink it. Cook with the inexpensive or the left over stuff.

Tarragon and Orange Sauce
Makes 3 cups

1 cup chicken stock	*2 Tbs tarragon*
2 cups orange juice	*½ cup dry white wine*
Zest from 1 orange	*3 Tbs roux (see page 57)*
1 tsp turmeric	*1 Tbs molasses*

Place chicken stock on medium high heat and cook until reduced by ½. Add the orange juice, tarragon, turmeric, white wine, and cook for an additional 3 minutes. Add roux, 1 Tbs at a time, and stir until desired thickness. Add zest just before serving. If it gets too thick, add more orange juice. If it is too thin, add more roux. You can use this sauce on lots of dishes. We use it to nap the plate or ladle over a sliced pork loin. It's also great on ham, chicken, and even works as a sauce for pasta or egg noodles.

When you are using this sauce for roasted pork, mix about ½ cup of the pan drippings to the sauce for some additional flavoring. Same with roasted chicken.

Seafood

Fried Calamari
Serves 4

1 lb calamari, cartilage removed, cleaned and chopped into large pieces	2 eggs, whisked
	½ cup fine bread crumbs
2 cups buttermilk	½ cup olive oil
½ cup flour	Salt and pepper to taste

Place the cut calamari into a bowl with buttermilk and let sit overnight in the refrigerator. This will tenderize the calamari like you won't believe.

Take pieces of calamari from the buttermilk, one at a time, and dredge first in the flour. Next dip the calamari into the whisked eggs, and finally into the bread crumbs. Heat oil in a in a heavy skillet over a medium high heat. Fry the breaded calamari until golden brown. Do not overcook or it will take on the texture of an eraser on a #2 pencil. When browned, place on a plate and sprinkle with salt and pepper.

I like to serve these yummy morsels with a shrimp cocktail sauce with a bit of horseradish mixed in. Lots of people like to serve it with a mayonnaise based tartar sauce, and still others like to use an Italian ragout. If your friends and family are anything like mine, you may need to triple this recipe.

Monkfish with Mushrooms and White Wine Sauce
Serves 4

2 pounds monkfish or any firm white fish	1 cup dry white wine
½ stick butter	Pinch of salt
8 mushrooms	Pinch of pepper
3 Tbs dried parsley	2 eggs, whisked
1 bunch scallions, trimmed and only the white part chopped	

Preheat oven to 400 degrees.

Butter an ovenproof dish big enough to hold the fish filets in a single layer. Thinly slice mushrooms, including the stems. Evenly place over the bottom of the buttered dish. Sprinkle dried parsley and chopped scallions over the mushrooms. Arrange the fish on top of this. Pour wine over fish and top with salt and pepper. Bake covered in a preheated 400 degree oven for 10 minutes. Remove the lid and baste the fish with the cooking liquid from the pan. Lower the oven temperature to 350 degrees and finish cooking, uncovered, for an additional 10 minutes. Make sure fish flakes easily, if so remove from oven, if not cook some more.

Drain off the cooking liquid into a small sauce pan. Add remaining butter and cook over medium heat until butter is melted. In a separate bowl whisk the eggs. Slowly add the cooking liquid from the sauce pan, one spoon at a time, to the whisked eggs. Be careful not to add too fast as it will cook the eggs. When the eggs are hot through and through, add the egg and juice mixture back into the sauce pan. Cook over low heat until you have a sauce the consistency of a hollandaise sauce. Pour over the fish. Now, taaa daaa, get out your blow torch. I love this part. So will any man in the house. Set to medium high and torch the top of the fish until the sauce begins to brown. Serve immediately.

Quick Mussels
Serves 4

4 lbs mussels	2 cups clam juice (or 1 cup clam juice and 1 cup fish stock)
4 cups water	

Before cooking, vigorously scrub each mussel, washing away any sand or grime that may still be attached. It may or may not have a little beard, anything from a Van Dyke to the Santa Clause kind. Grasp the beard and pull it tightly away from the shell, then yank it down towards the hinge at the bottom of the mussel. It should come loose. Note that this will kill the mussel as well, so do not do this ahead of time. Mussels need to be immediately cooked after removal of the beard.

In a large pan bring the clam juice, water, and fish stock (if you've used it) to a rolling boil. Add mussels and cook for just a few minutes, just until you see the shells open up. Remove the shellfish from the water and discard any that don't open. The ones that don't open have already died and could be toxic if eaten. Do NOT feed them to your cat, dog, chickens, monkeys, or ferrets.

When cooking mussels - less is best. Less cooking time and less mucking about with complicated sauces. Keep it simple.

Chef's notes - My favorite mussels are the green lipped ones from New Zealand. When I lived in Australia we could buy them in a gallon bucket for about 4 dollars - ahhhh the good ole days. Black lipped mussels have a much stronger flavor and are usually smaller.

When you buy mussels, ask your fish monger to see the tag – by law all fresh shellfish should have an accompanying tag. The tag will give you valuable information on the origin of the shellfish. Make sure you are comfortable with the country of origin. All shellfish are not the same. They are not all raised in the best habitat. Ask your fish monger. If you aren't able to get fresh mussels, buy them frozen on the half shell or completely shelled. These will already be cleaned before the freezing process. Pull them out of the freezer just before cooking and drop them frozen into the boiling water. Do not, I repeat, do not let them defrost first on the counter. Shellfish spoil fast! They have to be either very cold or very hot - do not eat it if it seems to be at room temperature. Shell fish poisoning is very bad. Repeat, very bad.

Quick Tomato Sauce Suitable for any Shell Fish
Makes about 2 cups

Zest and juice from 1 lemon	Pinch of Pepper
2 diced tomatoes (or 1 14-oz can of chopped tomatoes with juice)	½ tsp crushed red pepper flakes (or ½ tsp Tabasco sauce)
2 cloves garlic, crushed	2 Tbs bread crumbs
Pinch of Salt	1 tsp prepared horseradish

Place all ingredients in a bowl with sides high enough that an emersion blender can be used to incorporate the ingredients into a sauce. You can whip this up in a few seconds. Use canned tomatoes including the juice if you don't have any fresh tomatoes.

Chef's notes – Other sauces that go great with shellfish include Garlic Aioli (chopped garlic in mayonnaise), Clarified Butter (aka drawn butter) (see page 62), Citrus Sauce (see page 62), and Diablo Sauce (see page 63).

Octopus in Paprika Sauce
Serves 8

4 lbs fresh octopus	¼ cup extra virgin olive oil
6 quarts slightly salted water	6 bay leaves
1 large onion peeled and coarsely chopped	1 Tbs smoked paprika
	3 Tbs roux (see page 57)
Fresh ginger, about the size of your thumb, peeled and thinly sliced	½ tsp cayenne pepper
	Salt and pepper to taste
6 juniper berries	
12 cloves garlic, crushed and peeled	

In a soup pot, over medium high heat, bring salted water to a rolling boil. Add the onion, ginger, juniper berries, and 4 garlic cloves, skins removed, to the water. In the meantime, cut the fresh octopus into one inch pieces, including the mantle. Remove the beak if it is still intact. Add the octopus and immediately drop the water to a slow simmer. Cook for approximately 1 to 1 ½ hours or until the octopus is tender. As soon as the octopus is done, put aside to cool. Discard cooking water, retaining 4 cups for the sauce.

Heat the oil, 3 bay leaves, and remaining crushed garlic in a large heavy frying pan over medium heat. Cook until the garlic is browned. Remove garlic and set aside. Add paprika to the skillet and sauté until the spice starts to release its oils. Be careful not to burn the paprika as it goes from almost done to burnt in an instant. Add 3 cups of the retained cooking liquid and 2 tablespoons of roux. Stir constantly until the liquid starts to thicken. Add more roux as needed to thicken the cooking water until a light sauce is formed. If it gets too thick, just add some more of the cooking liquid as needed. Add the crushed garlic and the octopus back to the sauce to thoroughly heat and coat. Add cayenne pepper, a pinch at a time, checking for spicy heat. Add salt and pepper to taste. Can be served hot or cold.

Red Snapper in Red Wine

Serves 4

2 lbs red snapper	*½ cup fish stock*
3 thick slices of bacon	*Zest and juice from 1 lemon*
2 pounds new red potatoes cut into ovals, ½ inch thick.	*1 tsp chopped garlic*
	3 Tbs chilled butter cut into 3 pieces
½ cup diced onions	*½ cup chopped fresh parsley*
1/3 cup clarified butter	*Salt and pepper*
2 cups dry red wine	

Cook bacon in skillet until crisp, remove bacon and set aside. Reserve the bacon fat. Cut potatoes into ½ inch rounds, boil for about 10 minutes, drain and pat dry. Next sauté the potatoes in reserved bacon fat until they are golden brown on both sides.

Add onions and cook until they just begin to wilt. Remove potatoes and onions to platter and set aside. Pour off the rest of the pan drippings. Add 1/3 cup clarified butter to pan and cook on medium high, add fish fillets and sauté 2 - 3 minutes on each side. Place fillets on platter with potatoes and onions, and hold in a warm oven with the door ajar.

Pour off the clarified butter from the skillet. Add wine to the skillet and deglaze the pan. Add fish stock, lemon juice and zest, garlic, and cook until liquid is reduced by half. Whisk in the chilled butter; do not bring to a boil, heat just until the butter is melted. Add salt and pepper to taste. Nap each serving plate with this sauce and arrange fish, potato and onions on each plate. Top with reserved chopped bacon and chopped parsley.

Roasted Red Snapper with Fennel and Bell Peppers
Serves 4

1 medium sized whole red snapper (about 2 pounds)	8 cloves garlic, mashed, peeled, and minced
½ cup olive oil	1 lemon
1 Tbs honey	1 orange
3 Tbs fennel seeds	1 lime
1 tsp thyme	2 fennel bulbs, sliced thinly
1 tsp oregano	1 red onion, sliced thinly
1 tsp paprika	1 red bell pepper. sliced thinly
Salt and pepper to taste	1 green bell pepper, sliced thinly

Preheat oven to 375 degrees.

This recipe is a lot less work than it appears. Combine the oil, honey, spices, garlic in a large mixing bowl. Cut the lime, orange, and lemon in half. Juice and zest one half of each citrus fruit. Add to the mixing bowl. Retain the other halves. Add all the vegetables to the oil mixture and fold together until they are all thoroughly coated. Brush a small amount of the oil from the oil and veggie mixture onto a sheet pan. Place the fish on the pan and stuff the inside of the fish with the vegetable mixture. Take the remaining citrus halves and slice thinly. Take the sliced lemons, limes and oranges and make a fish scale pattern on top of the fish. Pour the remaining liquid over the fish, cover with foil and cook for about 30 minutes. Over cooked fish is a no - no, so keep a close eye on your remote thermometer, about 125 -130 degrees is usually done, but make sure the fish flakes when probed with a fork.

This is one of those beautiful dishes you can make a day ahead of time. Follow directions all the way though putting citrus "fish scales" on the fish. Then refrigerate until ready to cook. About an hour before you want to eat, pull the fish from the refrigerator and let come to room temperature. Preheat the oven to 375 degrees and cook for about a half an hour until the fish flakes easily.

This dish always elicits ohhs and ahhhs from your guests. The nice part about this dish is you can make it ahead of time and still be able to entertain and enjoy your guests.

Salmon in Parchment Paper
Serves 4

2 lbs Salmon filets	9 cloves garlic, crushed, peeled, and chopped
1 yellow onion, peeled and chopped	
1 red onion, peeled and chopped	3 Tbs olive oil
1 red bell pepper, skinned and chopped finely	1 Tbs red pepper flakes
	Salt and pepper to taste
1 green bell pepper, skinned and chopped finely	2 sprigs of fresh dill
	2 sprigs of fresh rosemary
3 tomatoes seeded, peeled, and chopped finely (or 1 14-oz can chopped tomatoes, drain away juices)	

Place onion, peppers and tomatoes under broiler and cook until they just start to blacken. Remove vegetables from oven. Remove skins from bell peppers. Remove skins and seeds from tomatoes. Dice all vegetables into small pieces.

Reduce oven to 350 degrees.

Heat oil over moderate heat in a large skillet. Add onion, garlic, red and green bell peppers, tomatoes, red pepper flakes, dill, and rosemary. When the vegetables are al dente, remove from skillet and set aside. Add the salmon filets to the same pan and brown for 3 minutes on each side.

Lay parchment paper on a flat surface. In the middle of the paper place a serving sized piece of salmon filet and ¼ of the cooked veggies and other ingredients. Wrap and fold paper around fish and vegetables making a little cooking packet. Make 4 packets, one for each serving. Place on a cookie sheet and cook in oven at 350 degrees for approximately 30 minutes.

Serve by placing a fish packet on each plate for each guest. Bring to the table still wrapped up in its little paper packet. Be careful; tell your guests that when opening up the parchment paper the released steam can be quite hot.

Chef's notes - When I lived in the South Pacific we would usually cook fish and shellfish in banana leaves. The fish would emerge moist, flavorful and infused with the herbs that we added to the little packets that were thrown into the communal cooking pit. Banana leaves are few and far between here in the states. However, this parchment paper wrapping method is a good alternative cooking method that mimics those South Pacific island dishes that delighted me when I was just a young sprout. By utilizing parchment paper as a substitute for banana leaves we can still experience this wonderful cooking technique. Everything comes out moist and flavorful.

Sautéed Sole with Butter and Capers
Serves 4

4 large filets of sole	2 Tbs clarified butter
½ cup flour	Juice and zest of 1 lemon
2 eggs, whisked	¼ cup dry white wine
½ cup breadcrumbs	¼ cup capers

Dip the fish first in the flour, then in the whisked eggs, and then into the breadcrumbs. This is called a *bound breading*. Place breaded fish into a heated skillet with clarified butter and sauté for 3 to 5 minutes a side. Add more clarified butter as needed. When browned nicely on each side, remove and hold on a heated platter. Deglaze the pan with the wine and lemon juice and scrape up all the crusty bits left in the pan, add the capers and lemon zest and pour all over the fillets of sole. Serve immediately.

Chef's notes - Most fish dishes can be quickly prepared in a sauté pan with butter and a few spices. Keeping it simple allows the fresh fish taste to come to the forefront. If a fish has been so smothered in sauces, you can't really taste the fish. This simple recipe is one of my favorites and can be used with about any kind of fish.

Seafood Stew
Serves 4 to 6

3 cups basic tomato sauce (see page 60)	1 pound fish, cut into pieces (try sea bass, rock cod, halibut, or any firm fish)
2 cups fish stock (see page 41)	12 - 14 clams, cleaned and washed
Zest and juice from 1 lemon	12 - 14 green lipped mussels, cleaned and washed
2 tsp red pepper flakes	12 - 14 large shrimp, with shells on
1 Tbs parsley flakes	12 – 14 scallops, cut in half
1 Tbs sweet basil	1 whole crab, cut into pieces
1/3 cup dry white wine	1 cup chicken stock
Pinch of saffron threads	3 Tbs chopped garlic
½ cup water	

Heat basic tomato sauce with fish stock, chicken stock, chopped garlic, lemon juice and zest, spices, and wine. Make tea from saffron and ½ cup of warm water. Add to broth after steeping for 10 minutes. Now add all the fish and cleaned

shellfish and cook for 15 minutes. Make sure the clams and mussels open their shells, discarding those that did not open. Do not overcook, or the shell fish will get tough.

Ladle stew into serving bowls, making sure each bowl has some of each of the different fish/shellfish available. Serve hot with a crusty bread for dipping.

> Chef's note – In the interest of time, if you are not able to make your own fish stock, you can substitute store bought clam juice. Sometimes you can buy fish stock from your local seafood restaurant, give them a call and ask if they sell it. Very few grocery stores ever carry fish stock, you may be able to find some in an Asian market. The clam juice is a reasonable substitute, but the real deal fish stock is a hard flavor to duplicate or substitute. If you are trying to really impress a group of friends or guests, make the fish stock.

Chicken

Chicken Adobo
Serves 6

6 chicken breasts, with bones and skin	1/3 cup red wine vinegar
4 dried Ancho chili peppers	½ tsp dried oregano
1 large onion, chopped fine	Pinch of cinnamon
4 limes, juice and zest	¼ tsp dried coriander
8 cloves garlic, crushed, peeled, and minced	¼ cup olive oil
1 tsp cumin	1 14-oz can chopped tomatoes, including juice
½ tsp dried thyme	½ cup chicken stock (see page 38)
½ tsp red pepper flakes	½ cup brown sugar
Half a bunch of fresh cilantro	2 Tbs roux (see page 57)

Cover the dried chilies with 2 cups of boiling water and let soak for ½ hour. Split the chilies and remove stems and seeds. Place cleaned chilies, onion, lemon juice and zest, minced garlic, cumin, thyme, red pepper flakes, cilantro, vinegar, oregano, cinnamon, coriander, olive oil, canned tomatoes and juice, ½ cup chicken stock, ½ cup chili water, and brown sugar into the food processor and process until a paste-like marinade is made. Save and refrigerate an additional cup of the chili water for use later when making the sauce for the chicken Place chicken breasts into a bowl and cover with the marinade paste. Cover and refrigerate for at least 1 day, turning the meat to keep the chicken in contact with the marinade. If you have the time, two days is even better.

Remove the meat from the marinade and brown in a heavy cast iron Dutch oven or skillet. Reduce heat to a simmer. Remove the meat and set aside in a covered bowl in the refrigerator. Add the remaining marinade to the pan with the additional cup of saved chili water. Cook until it becomes slightly thickened, like gravy. Add roux, a small amount at a time to get to the right constancy. (Water can be added as well if it gets too thick.) Add the chicken back to the sauce, cover, and simmer for 1 ½ to 2 hours. Serve immediately over rice.

Cheezy Chicken Breast in White Wine Sauce
Serves 4

2 whole chicken breasts, halved, bone in	1 cup half and half (whole milk works well too)
2 eggs	½ small white onion, diced
½ cup water	½ clove garlic, minced
Pinch of salt	3 Tbs dried parsley
Pinch of coarse ground black pepper	1 dried bay laurel leaf
¾ cup flour	2 ribs chopped celery 1 whole lemon, juiced and zested
¾ cup fine bread crumbs	4 slices Swiss or Provolone cheese
4 Tbs butter	
½ cup white wine	

Preheat oven to 375 degrees.

Whisk the egg and water together in a bowl that will accommodate the chicken pieces one at a time. Mix salt and pepper into flour and place in small pie pan. Place bread crumbs in a separate small pie pan. Dip the chicken breast into the flour, covering all sides. Dip into the egg wash, make sure the egg mixture coats the whole piece, take a spoon and drizzle it on here and there if you have to. Now take chicken and press into bread crumbs, set aside and chill for at least ½ hour.

Melt 3 Tbs butter in heavy skillet, sauté chicken on each side until lightly browned. Add more butter as required. Remove from the pan and set aside. Deglaze pan with white wine, scraping up all the crusty parts with a wooden spoon. Now add the cream, onion, garlic, parsley, bay leaf, celery; simmer 10 minutes.

Place chicken breasts, skin side up, in casserole or baking dish. One layer only. Place a piece of Swiss cheese on top of each piece. Strain the cream sauce, so it is lump free and all the vegetables are removed as much as possible. Whisk in lemon juice and zest to the sauce. Spoon sauce all around the chicken pieces and bake uncovered at 375 degrees for about 15 minutes or until the cheese is melted. Serve hot.

Chicken with White Wine Sauce in Rice Pie Crusts
Serves 6

Rice crust for the pie

4 cups long grain white rice	1 Tbs olive oil
3 cups water	½ cup freshly grated parmesan cheese
Salt and pepper to taste	4 egg whites, whisked
1 cup chicken stock (see page 38)	

Preheat oven to 350 degrees.

Place rice, 3 cups of water and one cup of chicken stock in a large pot on the stove over medium heat. Add salt and pepper to taste. Boil for approximately 10 minutes, cover and cook an additional 5 minutes or until done. Remove from heat and cool.

When cool, add ½ cup parmesan cheese, one tablespoon olive oil and beaten egg whites, mix together. In a well buttered pie pan pat rice mixture into pan, making sure to bring the rice up the sides to the top of the pie pan.

Depending on your elevation, temperature, and how good you are at measuring, you might have quite a bunch of the rice mixture left over. You can refrigerate the mixture or build another pie crust. Remember this is supposed to be fun and there are no absolutes in cooking.

Pie Filling

3 pounds boneless chicken cut into medium sized pieces	1 tsp thyme
	1 tsp dried tarragon
2 strips bacon	5 cloves garlic, crushed and chopped fine
1 Tbs olive oil	
1 red bell pepper charred, seeds removed, chopped fine	½ cup sweet white wine
	1 cup chicken stock
2 yellow onions, chopped fine	3 Tbs roux (see page 57)
½ cup pearl onions, peeled	½ cup parmesan cheese
1 tsp paprika	

Preheat oven to 350 degrees.

Cook the bacon until crispy. Remove and set aside. Add olive oil to bacon fat. Add the chicken, sauté until the pieces of chicken are cooked and browned all over. Add the bell pepper, onions, spices, and garlic. Sauté over medium heat and work on getting a nice brown crust on the bottom of the pan. Remove all the chicken and vegetables from the pan and set aside. Deglaze the pan with the wine. Get a wooden spoon and work the yummy burnt bits off the bottom of the pan. Add 1 cup of chicken stock, the roux, and cook until the sauce thickens. Add the cooked chicken

and all the vegetables back to the skillet with the thickened sauce. Add the ½ cup of parmesan cheese. Add the retained chopped bacon to the filling mixture.

Pour the chicken pie filling into the rice pie crust. Bake pie in preheated 350 degree oven and cook for about 20 minutes, or until the pie filling is bubbling. Of course, you can always make this chicken pie with a regular pastry shell as well.

Chef's notes - My son called me the other day and informed me that he had been diagnosed with an allergic reaction to wheat flour. It seems there are a lot of people out there who are allergic to gluten found in wheat flour. This rice pie crust is a great way to have a viable alternative to regular flour pie crust.

Chicken and Sausage Paella
Serves 8

3 cups uncooked rice, long grain	¼ tsp saffron
4 Tbs cooking oil	2 Tbs paprika
1 medium onion, coarsely chopped	1 ½ lbs cooked chicken
½ cup whole peeled garlic	1 ½ lbs cooked sausage
6 cups chicken stock	1 cup frozen peas

Preheat oven to 400 degrees.

Place oil in 17-18 inch paella pan or large oven proof skillet. Heat over medium high heat; add chopped onions and whole garlic. Sauté until garlic and onions are slightly browned. Remove onions and garlic and set aside. Add rice to the same pan, stir and sauté rice until each rice kernel is coated with oil and rice beings to toast. In the meantime, place the saffron threads into one cup of the chicken stock and let steep for 15 minutes.

While saffron is steeping, add remaining chicken stock to paella pan with the sautéed rice. Reintroduce the sautéed onions and garlic to the pan, add paprika. Bring the rice and chicken stock mixture to a slow boil, reduce heat, add saffron infused chicken stock, cover and simmer until most of the stock is absorbed by the rice, about 20 minutes. Add cooked chicken and sausage. Add frozen peas. Fold all ingredients together. Place, uncovered, into a preheated 400 degree oven for 30 minutes. A light crust will form on the bottom of the paella pan. This is called the "sucarret" and is the sign of a well made paella. It is very similar to the crust you get when making hash brown potatoes. When the paella comes out of the oven take a spatula and loosen and scrape up the sucarret from the bottom of the pan and mix it in with the rest of the paella for a crunch nutty texture and taste.

Chef's notes - We have won several paella contests with this exact recipe. Most people in the United States think paella is a seafood dish. It is an anything you want to put in it dish! There are a great many recipes for paella calling out for a short grained rice, arborio is the most common, but we have found that the long grained rice works best for us. It is also easier to find. The short grained rice absorbs more liquid and ends up being too wet for our liking. Also note that a paella pan is a specialized pan. It is very flat with a large surface area for cooking. Sometimes the bottom of the pan has been dimpled so as to help with the formation of the sucarret. The dimples trap some steam and help form the crust. If you don't have a paella pan, a large cast iron pan works well. Add any protein or vegetables that you have. It is a glamorous way to use up leftovers, which is how it originated in Spain in the first place. In the USA, we make casseroles using leftovers, in Spain and the Basque country, they make paella.

Coq Au Vin

Serves 5

5 pounds senior citizen chicken leg quarters (legs attached to thighs)	*3 cloves garlic, crushed*
	1 pound pearl onions
4 strips bacon or fat back	*10 medium sized whole mushrooms*
½ cup butter, room temperature	*1 cup chicken stock*
3 Tbs all purpose flour	*5 cups cooked rice or noodles*
4 cups dry red wine (I like Cab or Zin)	*4 Tbs roux (see page 57)*
Bouquet garni made with pepper corns, bay leaf, celery tops, and sprigs of parsley	

Preheat oven to 300 degrees.

Place bacon in an uncovered Dutch oven over medium heat. Fry bacon until it is crispy and the fat has rendered out. (Remember do not do this naked!) Remove bacon and add butter. Dust chicken pieces with the flour, and then fry in the bacon fat and butter until browned. Remove from pan and set aside.

Deglaze the pan with half the wine and scrape up all the yummy crunchy bits. Add bouquet garni, garlic, remaining wine, pearl onions, mushrooms, chopped bacon and chicken stock. Mix together on the stove top.

Re-introduce the browned chicken back into the pan. Cover and place in preheated oven at 300 degrees for at least 2 hours, or until the chicken is just ready to fall off the bone. Remove bouquet garni. Remove chicken from the pot and place over rice or noodles. Place the pot back on the stove top, heat on high and add enough of the roux to thicken the juices. Ladle the sauce over the chicken. Serve piping hot.

Chef's notes – Let's talk about chicken. Most chickens you buy at the store today come out of a factory farm and are kept in close confinement without the ability to run around chasing bugs and getting buff. Consequently, they are tender and juicy but they lack the real chicken flavor that you would get from a chicken right out of the barnyard that has spent its life dodging foxes, coyotes, and farmer Jones. But, if you have ever tried to cook a chicken right off the farm or an older hen or rooster you know firsthand that they are as tough as my old pair of clogs. So how can we prepare juicy, tasty chicken dishes that are also fork tender? Long cooking times combined with a wet cooking method at a relatively low temperature will tame even the oldest birds.

The Coq Au Vin recipe is a classic one and was originally used to cook the old, tough rooster that was way past his prime. These days, unless you live on a farm, roosters are hard to come by but there is a very good alternative: old laying hens. They are cheap and tasty and can be found at your local butchers. Usually pack-aged frozen as leg quarters in ten pound bags. If your butcher doesn't have them in stock he can usually order them. Less than a dollar a pound they are a super value and yummy.

Drunk Chicken
Serves 4

1 large whole chicken or 2 pounds leg and thigh meat	*½ tsp cayenne pepper*
1 Tbs extra virgin olive oil	*8 cloves garlic crushed and then chopped very fine*
4 Tbs canola oil	*1 Tbs paprika*
3 cans of beer	*1 whole medium onion*
Bouquet garni, made with 6 whole peppercorns, celery tops, sprigs of parsley, 3 bay leaves	*2 large carrots cut in quarters*
	1 Tbs roux (see page 57)
	Salt and pepper to taste

Preheat oven to 350 degrees.

In a large, heavy Dutch oven or skillet cook the olive oil and the canola oil over a medium heat. Add the chicken and brown on both sides. Deglaze the pan using 1 can of beer. Place the bouquet garni, minced garlic, cayenne pepper, paprika, onion and carrots in the cavity of the whole chicken. If using leg and thigh meat, place all of the ingredients in the pan and place the chicken pieces on top. Using the remaining 2 cans of beer cover everything and cook uncovered on the stove over a medium heat for approximately 45 minutes. The liquid should have evaporated by half. Cover the pan and place in a 350 degree oven for approximately 1 hour.

Remove from the oven, remove cover and place on medium heat on the stove top. Remove the chicken and set aside. Remove the bouquet garni and discard. Remove the cooked carrot and onion from out of the chicken and place back into the cooking pot. Using an emersion blender, wiz the cooked carrot and onion with the juices together into a sauce. Add the roux and, just as the sauce thickens, put in the chicken. Add salt and pepper to taste.

Can be served over rice or noodles and I promise even your teetotaling guests will love it.

Garlic Chicken with Almond Sauce
Serves 8

4 lbs cut up chicken	*8 garlic cloves smashed and then minced*
Pinch of saffron threads	*2 Tbs fresh cilantro*
½ cup red wine	*½ tsp turmeric*
½ cup olive oil	*3 Tbs almond paste (see page 58)*
2 Tbs chopped celery	*1 cup finely chopped almonds*
2 Tbs chopped onion	*½ cup pimento stuffed olives, whole*
2 Tbs chopped carrots	*4 Tbs roux (see page 57)*
1 cup white wine	

Preheat oven to 350 degrees.

Soak the chicken in heavily salted water for at least 3 hours then remove and pat dry. Add the saffron to the red wine and set aside.

Add the oil to a Dutch oven and cook on medium heat. When the oil is hot, brown the chicken on all sides. Remove the chicken and set aside. Add celery, onion, and carrots to the Dutch oven. Sauté to create a mirepoix (see page 17). Deglaze the pan with the white wine. Add garlic, saffron infused red wine, cilantro, turmeric, almond paste, almonds, chicken and olives. Cover the Dutch oven and place into a preheated 350 degree oven for 2 hours.

Remove the chicken from the pot and set aside. Stir the pan drippings well. Add roux to the pan drippings to thicken the sauce and pour over the chicken. Serve over egg noodles or rice.

Roasted Rosemary Chicken
Serves 6

5 lbs leg quarters	*½ cup kosher salt*
4 large unpeeled carrots cut into long pieces	*2 Tbs granulated garlic*
	1 Tbs coarse ground pepper
1 yellow onion, peeled and coarsely chopped	*1 Tbs paprika*
	3 Tbs dried rosemary
½ cup white wine	*5 sprigs of fresh rosemary used for garnish*
½ cup water	

Preheat oven to 350 degrees.

In a roasting pan place unpeeled carrots, cut lengthwise, and coarsely chopped onions. Add leg quarters, placing directly on top of the onions and carrots. Chicken should be placed skin side up. Do not place chicken pieces on top of one another - one layer only. Pour white wine and water over chicken pieces.

Mix all dry ingredients together making a spice mix. Sprinkle each piece with approximately 1 tsp of spice mixture on each leg quarter. Cover and cook for 2 hours. Skin should be golden brown when finished. Remove carrots and onions from the pan and place on platter and top with the cooked chicken.

Garnish with fresh rosemary sprigs.

Chef's notes - When buying leg quarters, find the biggest, baddest, oldest chicken you can find. Ask your butcher or meat guy or gal at the butcher counter for some of these older bigger birds. You are going to cook this for a few hours, the connective tissue in the older chicken helps hold it together better. Younger chickens are too tender and won't give you the "fall off the bone" quality you want with this dish. Most markets will sell these older chicken leg quarters frozen in 10 lb bags. Defrost enough to separate the pieces of chicken, use ½ the bag. Save the other ½ for another time placing the still frozen chicken back into the freezer. Be careful not to totally defrost all the chicken, you don't want to thaw it completely and then re-freeze.

Also, after cooking the chicken you will find a wonderful broth at the bottom of the pan. Strain it through a cheese cloth lined colander and refrigerate overnight. The next day you can easily remove any chicken fat that will have risen to the top and have a wonderful chicken broth available to make something else. When cold, the broth will be like gelatin because of the bones from the chicken, once you heat it, it will melt and be a delicious broth. It will keep, if refrigerated, for about 10 days. You can also freeze it, but be sure to date and label it.

Pork

Bell Pepper and Pork Pie
Serves 12

3 lbs lean pork roast cut into bite sized portions	2 Tbs chopped garlic
½ tsp dried basil	½ cup olive oil, divided
½ tsp paprika	1 cup wine (your choice, dry)
¼ cup minced parsley	1 cup chicken stock
1 cup pearl onions	1 cup beef stock
½ cup onions, chopped	2 Tbs molasses
6 medium carrots, cut diagonally in 2 inch pieces	2 Tbs roux
3 bell peppers, seeded and sliced into ribbons	Pastry for 2 9-inch pie crusts (see page 54)
Salt and pepper to taste	Egg wash

Preheat oven to 350 degrees.

In large bowl toss cut pieces of pork loin, basil, paprika, parsley, onions, carrots, bell peppers, salt and pepper and garlic with ¼ cup olive oil. Cover bowl and marinate in the refrigerator for at least 2 hours, over-night is better. Turn pork over frequently to distribute the marinade.

Heat on medium high heat, ¼ cup olive oil in heavy skillet and add marinated carrots, sauté a few minutes till they are al dente. Remove and set aside. Sauté remaining marinated vegetables and garlic until tender or until the onions are translucent but not yet browned. Remove from the skillet and set aside. Add the pieces of pork and the rest of the marinade. Cook over high heat, turning the pork pieces as they brown. When all the meat is nicely browned, remove and add the wine to deglaze the pan. Add the chicken and beef stock and cook over medium high heat to reduce the liquid by half. Add the molasses. Mix well. Taste it! Add additional salt and pepper to taste.

Add roux and cook until thickened. Reintroduce all ingredients and simmer for 45 minutes. Set aside.

Make pie dough. Spoon the pork and vegetable mixture into 2 pie pans, top with rolled out pie dough. Cut slits into the pastry top to vent while cooking. Brush entire pie with egg wash for a wonderful golden color. Bake in preheated 350 degree oven for about 45 minutes, or until the crust is a golden brown. Remove from oven and let cool for at least 15 minutes. Serve warm.

Herb Encrusted Pork Loin
Serves 8

4 lbs pork loin (not tenderloin)	½ cup fresh mint, chopped
10 whole garlic cloves, peeled and crushed	1 tsp salt
2 Tbs dried parsley	1 tsp freshly ground pepper
2 Tbs ground sage	1 Tbs garlic powder
2 Tb dried rosemary	1 Tbs onion powder
2 Tbs dried basil	¼ cup olive oil

Preheat oven to 350 degrees.

Crush peeled garlic cloves together with all the dried and fresh herbs in a mortar and pestle. (You can substitute fresh herbs for any of the above, or add others that you like). Add olive oil and continue to crush. You will end up with a paste. Rub paste all over the pork loin. Place on baking sheet, fat side up. Put any extra paste on the top. Bake in preheated oven for approximately 1 ½ hours. Check with instant read thermometer at 1 hour. You want internal temperature to be at least 160 degrees. Set aside to rest, it will continue cooking. After about 15 minutes slice and serve.

Chef's notes – Try serving this dish with two or three different sauces from our sauce section. We especially like the Orange Tarragon Sauce (see page 66) and the Reduced Merlot Sauce (see page 66). It's fun to give your guests the option of experiencing a couple of different, tasty, yummy sauces.

Red Cabbage and Pork Chops
Serves 4

4 large bone-in pork chops	2 tart green apples, with peels left on, cored and sliced
Pinch of salt	1 yellow onion, thinly sliced
Pinch of pepper	1 clove garlic, minced
2 Tbs bacon fat	Pinch of thyme
2 Tbs butter	2 Tbs balsamic vinegar
1 medium sized red or purple cabbage	2 Tbs sugar
1 Tbs fennel seeds	

Salt and pepper both sides of the pork chops. In a heavy pan with a lid, brown the pork chops on both sides in the bacon fat and butter. Set pork chops

aside and refrigerate. Slice cabbage into very thin slices (like coleslaw) and sauté in the remaining hot fat for 10 minutes. Cover, cook for an additional 5 minutes.

Meanwhile, take fennel seeds and place in a small dry skillet. Cook over medium high heat until the oils release and you can really begin to smell the licorice aroma. Add the cooked fennel seeds to the cabbage. Add sliced apples and onions, and mince garlic to the cabbage. Add the thyme, vinegar, and sugar. Fold all the ingredients together in the pan. Cover and cook for 1 hour over low heat. You may need to add a little water (¼ to ½ cup) to keep moist. A half hour before serving, return the pork chops to the pan, on top of the cabbage and apples and cook, covered, for 30 minutes longer or until pork chops are heated through. Transfer to individual plates, or serve Basque style – on one large platter for the entire table.

Rolled Pork Loin, with Sage and Dried Fruit Stuffing
Serves 8

12" whole pork loin (approximately 4 lbs), butterflied – do not use pork tenderloin	6 whole garlic cloves, peeled and cut in half
1 stick unsalted butter	3 cups day old bread cubes
1 medium yellow onion, chopped	¾ cup chicken stock (see page 38)
4 celery ribs, cut into ½ inch pieces	¼ cup dried sweetened dried cranberries or raisins
2 Tbs dry sage	½ cup chopped dried apricots
1 bay leaf	½ cup water

Preheat oven to 350 degrees.

In a large skillet melt the butter, add chopped onions, celery, sage, bay leaf, and halved peeled garlic cloves. Cook until the onions and celery are just limp, not translucent. (These ingredients will continue to cook when the pork loin roll is roasted.) Remove from heat and place in a large mixing bowl, add bread cubes, chicken stock, dried cranberries, and diced apricots. Mix well, incorporating all the ingredients together. Set aside to cool.

Butterfly the pork loin. To butterfly, take a deep breath and get your sharpest chef's knife (use whatever knife you are most comfortable with, but it has to be able to easily slice through the pork meat). Looking down at the pork loin, visualize in your head the roast divided into thirds down the length of the loin. Make one long, lengthwise slice along the first third from one end of the loin to the other. Make sure not to cut all the way through the loin as you make this slice. The depth of the cut should leave about an inch thick layer of meat at the bottom of the loin uncut. Allow that first third of meat to lay out flat while turning your knife to be parallel with the table.

Starting at the base of the first cut, slice the entire length of the loin horizontally, maintaining the one inch thickness, until you get about half way through the remaining roast. Now take your knife and cut the pork upward, leaving about an

inch at the top of the cut. Unfold the meat you've just cut. It should now be a rather flat piece of meat with a rectangular shape. At this point take a meat mallet and pound the pork filet to try to make it the same thickness from one end to the other. This pounding also breaks down some of the connective tissue and will make the meat more tender.

With your hands, spread the cooled stuffing mixture evenly, about ¾" thick, over the entire surface area of the butterflied roast, watch for the bay leaf which you now want to remove. Lift the roast slightly at one corner, and look at the bottom of your roast. You will find one side has a strip of fat on it. On the opposite side of this fat strip begin loosely rolling the meat around the stuffing like a jelly roll.

When the entire piece of pork has been rolled up, take chef's twine and tie the roll into place every few inches (otherwise as the bread swells during the cooking process it will unroll - it will still taste good, but it will look like a dog's breakfast). Place roast into roasting pan with ½ cup water and cover with foil. The water keeps the meat moist. Cook for one hour and remove foil. Continue cooking for approximately ½ hour more, letting the meat brown. Check with an instant read thermometer. The internal temperature needs to be at 150 degrees. It will continue cooking as it rests. Remove from oven and let rest 15 minutes before slicing. (The resting is important to keep the roll from falling apart as you slice it). Slice with an electric knife in ¾ inch slices.

Serve with Tarragon and Orange Sauce (see page 66).

Beef

Basque Shepherd's Pie
Serves 6

1 ½ lb cooked and cubed beef, chicken, pork, or lamb (or a combination of any of these)	1 cup sliced mushrooms
	2 cups beef stock
2 Tbs cooking oil	1 cup chicken stock
1 cup red wine	1 tsp dried thyme
2 large onions, coarsely chopped	1 tsp dried sage
3 carrots, cut into 1 inch pieces	Salt and pepper to taste
3 ribs celery, cut into 1 inch pieces	1 tsp Worcestershire sauce
3 cloves garlic	3 Tbs roux
½ cup pearl onions	3 cups garlic mashed potatoes (see page 27)
1 14-oz can of chopped tomatoes, with juice	½ cup shredded cheddar cheese

Preheat oven to 350 degrees.

Brown meat in heavy skillet or Dutch oven in 2 Tbs of cooking oil. Remove meat from pan and set aside and refrigerate. You can also use left-over cooked meat, cut into bite sized chunks.

After meat has been removed, deglaze the pan with wine and reduce liquid by half. Add veggies, canned tomatoes, mushrooms, beef stock, chicken stock, Worchestershire sauce, and spices and cook for an additional ½ hour. Add roux and cook until soup thickens, add more roux if you don't think it is thick enough. Now, add the bite sized pieces of cooked meat. Continue cooking until meat is heated through.

While the meat pie filling is cooking, make garlic mashed potatoes and set aside to cool.

Place meat pie filling into a large oven proof casserole dish. With your handy dandy ice cream scoop, scoop out the garlic mashed potatoes and place each potato scooped ball onto the top of the pie filling. Cover completely with potato scooped balls allowing at least one potato ball for each person. Sprinkle with shredded cheddar cheese.

Place into a preheated 350 degree oven on cookie sheet - because sometimes it bubbles over and makes a big mess in the oven. When the cheese is melted and beginning to brown, about 20 minutes, remove and serve hot.

Chef's notes - It is important to set the meat aside while making the rest of the pie filling because if you cook the meat for the entire time needed to develop the gravy and sauce with the vegetables, the meat will be way over cooked. It may even disappear into the sauce completely, especially something tender like lamb.

Beaten Flank Steak Rolls
Serves 4

2 lbs flank steak	1 lb cooked spinach
Dijon mustard	1 onion, thickly sliced
1 Tbs chopped garlic	2 Tbs butter
½ tsp tarragon	½ cup dry red wine
Salt and pepper	4 slices provolone cheese
4 pieces cooked bacon	½ cup beef stock

Preheat oven to 350 degrees.

Combine mustard, garlic, and tarragon. With a meat mallet, pound flank steak until it is about ¼ inch thick. Cut into four pieces approximately the same size. On a flat surface lay out all four pieces of steak and spread one side with the Dijon mustard mix. Sprinkle with salt and pepper. Add 1 slice of bacon to each steak, breaking in half so it fits on to the steak. Squeeze all the water out of the prepared spinach and spoon down the middle of each steak. Add a slice of cheese

and onions to each steak. Roll up each steak as a jellyroll, tucking in the ends and sides so the cheese won't leak out. Tie with cook's twine so the beef roll won't come apart.

Heat butter in heavy skillet, add each beef roll and brown on all sides. Place beef rolls in a baking dish, seam side down. Add wine and beef stock. Bake covered in a preheated 350 degree over for about 50 minutes. Serve hot with pan drippings.

Sometimes we thicken the pan drippings and add sliced mushrooms to ladle over the top of the beef rolls.

Beef Bourguignonne, Basque Style!
Serves 6

3 lbs round steak or any kind of stew meat, cut into bite sized pieces	*4 cups red wine*
½ lb bacon cut into 1 inch strips	*2 cups beef stock*
2 Tbs olive oil	*2 bay leaves*
3 Tbs butter	*Bouquet garni*
6 cloves crushed garlic	*2 Tbs Molasses*
2 Tbs all purpose flour	*½ lb pearl onions (use them frozen, no one can tell the difference, and they are a lot easier to keep on hand, usually less expensive and already peeled)*
1 large white or yellow onions, coarsely chopped	
4 large unpeeled carrots, cut into 1 inch pieces	*1 lb whole mushrooms*

Cook the bacon over medium heat in a large heavy bottomed pan or Dutch oven until it is crisp. Remove and set aside. Add cubed meat to bacon fat along with olive oil, butter, garlic and flour. Cook until the meat is thoroughly browned. Remove meat and set aside. Add chopped onions and cut carrots, brown these and then remove and set aside.

Deglaze the pan with wine. Cook wine until it is reduced by half. Add the beef stock, spices, bacon, meat, browned carrots and onions and molasses. Simmer approximately 2 ½ hours. Add still frozen pearl onions and mushrooms at the end.

Preheat oven to 400 degrees at this point. Place ovenproof casserole dish filled with the meat, juices and veggies into the oven for ½ hour. Remove the bouquet garni before serving. Serve over egg noodles.

Braised Oxtails
Serves 6

1 whole oxtail, approximately 7 pounds- cut into 3" segments	3 large tomatoes, seeded, peeled, and chopped (or 1 14 oz can chopped tomatoes with juice)
3 Tbs oil	1 bay leaf
1 onion chopped	1 sprig parsley, chopped (or 1 tsp dry)
1 leek - white part only - chopped	1 sprig thyme, chopped (or 1 tsp dry)
3 diced carrots	½ tsp salt
2 garlic cloves, chopped	½ tsp pepper
4 slices raw bacon, cut into 1" pieces	Pinch crushed red pepper flakes
5 Tbs brandy	Pinch ground cloves
½ cup water	Fresh parsley to garnish
½ cup red wine	
1 cup beef stock	

Wash the oxtail very well. Blanch all the pieces in boiling water for about 5 minutes and drain.

Heat the oil over medium heat in a large heavy-bottomed pot. Add the onion, leeks, carrots, garlic, and bacon. Sauté until onion is soft and bacon is browned but not crisp, about 5 minutes. Add the blanched oxtails and brown over medium heat, about 8 minutes more. Add the brandy, water, wine, beef stock, tomatoes, bay leaf, parsley, thyme, salt and pepper, red pepper flakes, and cloves. Cover and cook for approximately 2 hours. Check every ½ hour or so and add more water, wine or beef stock as needed. When the dish is finished, about ½ the liquid should be remaining. Remove oxtails from the pot.

Take an emersion blender and process all the juices, cooked veggies, and bacon together to make a rich sauce. It should not need to be thickened. Nap a platter with the sauce, arrange the oxtails and top with remaining sauce. Garnish with chopped fresh parsley or whole parsley sprigs.

Cook's notes – Oxtails sometimes are not available. Use lamb or beef shanks instead. The bone marrow from each of these will add the richness and thickening you need for the sauce.

Brewed Beef
Serves 6

3 pounds beef, cut into bite-sized pieces	*Pinch of each:*
1 stick butter	*Thyme*
3 medium yellow onions, sliced	*Basil*
2 tsp flour	*Parsley*
1 tsp sugar	*Celery salt*
½ cup beef stock	*1 can of beer*
1 whole bay leaf	*2 Tbs roux (see page 57)*

In a heavy-bottomed pan with a good fitting lid, melt butter and brown meat. Remove meat and set aside. Brown onions in the same pan and butter. Add flour and sugar and mix well. Add the beef stock, spices and beer. Mix well. Place the meat back into the same pan, cover and simmer for about 1 ½ hours. (If using a slow crockery cooker, place the browned meat and the other ingredients into the crock and cook on low for about 4 or 5 hours.)

When meat is tender, remove from juices and place on a heated serving platter. Add roux to meat juices in the pan and stir with a whisk. Cook until slightly thickened. Spoon a little sauce over the meat and offer a gravy boat with the remaining sauce at the table.

If you used your handy dandy crockery cooker, after cooking the meat, transfer the liquid to a sauce pan and follow the same directions to create the gravy. A crockery cooker simply cannot get hot enough to make good gravy.

Filet with Green Peppercorns
Serves 6

2 lbs filet mignon, cut into 1/3 lb steaks	*1 cup beef stock*
6 slices Basque bread	*1 Tbs fresh lemon juice*
2 cups heavy cream	*½ tsp salt*
½ cup extra virgin olive oil	*¼ cup medium dry Sherry*
½ cup brandy	*¼ cup green peppercorns, rinsed, drained*

Take kitchen twine and tie each steak into round compact steaks. Cut bread into rounds so that it just fits each steak, toast each round on each side. Set aside on serving platter. Keep at room temperature.

In a small sauce pan cook heavy cream and the beef stock until it is reduced by half, stirring occasionally. Chill in refrigerator. In the meantime, heat olive oil in heavy skillet over medium high heat. Arrange steaks in the skillet in one layer. Cook for 3 to 4 minutes on each side for rare meat. If you like it more well done, cook a little longer. Take steaks from the skillet and place one filet on top of each toast on the serving platter.

Drain off most of the oil in the skillet, leaving about 1Tbs. Deglaze the pan with the brandy. Add lemon juice, salt, and sherry, chilled beef stock and cream reduction. Bring to just below a boil, add peppercorns and simmer for 10 minutes. Spoon a small amount of sauce over each steak, putting the rest of the sauce in a gravy boat so your guests can add more if they want to.

Chef's notes - You can certainly use other cuts of meat with this same sauce, but choose something that is tender. Try it over hamburger patties. Dresses 'em up real nice.

Grilled & Roasted Beef
Serves 8 to 10

1 4 or 5 pound beef roast, boneless (inside top round is good)	*1 cup reduced merlot sauce (see page 66)*
1 cup dry rub (see page 63)	

Generously rub beef roast with the dry rub and let marinate over-night, or for at least 6 hours. Grill over hot coals on all sides for about an hour. While meat is grilling, preheat oven to 350 degrees.

Transfer grilled meat to a baking pan with about ½ inch water in the bottom and finish cooking in a 350 degree oven. Roast uncovered for 45 minutes, or until an instant read thermometer inserted into the thickest part is 125 -135 degrees for rare meat. Cook longer if you like your roast more well done. Remove from oven, cover loosely with foil to retain some heat, and let rest for 10 - 15 minutes. Transfer to cutting board and cut as thin as you can. I use a small electric meat slicer at the restaurant. There should be some juices in the bottom of the roasting pan. Add 1/3 cup pan drippings to the reduced merlot sauce and cook until well heated.

At the restaurant, the meat is placed on a warmed serving platter and napped with the merlot reduction sauce. Next to the meat, on the same platter, we arrange green beans almandine, cooked al dente and served Basque style to the whole table. Each person takes their portion of beef and beans. Offer additional sauce at the table.

Lamb

Braised Young Lamb with Cilantro and Lemons
Serves 6

3 lbs lamb shoulder cut into bite sized pieces	*2 Tbs chopped garlic*
1 tsp olive oil	*½ tsp salt*
¾ cup dry wine (your choice)	*½ tsp coarse ground pepper*
1 ½ tsp ground cumin	*1 lemon, sliced into wedges*
	2 Tbs chopped fresh cilantro

In heavy 12 inch skillet, over medium heat, brown the lamb pieces in olive oil. Stir in the wine, (drink some too), cumin, garlic, salt and pepper. Cover and simmer for about 30 minutes. Add some more wine and the lemon wedges, cover and continue cooking over high heat for about 30 minutes. Stir gently until the sauce reduces and thickens. Serve over hot noodles with pan sauce and chopped fresh cilantro.

Leg of Lamb with Lemony Garlic Sauce
Serves 5 – 6

3 lbs leg of lamb	*6 cloves garlic, crushed*
2 lemons, zested and juiced	*1 tsp salt*
½ cup extra virgin olive oil	*1 tsp coarse ground pepper*

Place leg of lamb in shallow roasting pan. Whisk lemon juice and zest, crushed garlic, and olive oil together until emulsified. Pour over leg of lamb and refrigerate at least 2 hours, turn every ½ hour. Or make a day ahead and marinate

overnight in the fridge turning whenever you think about it (but at least 4 times). Be sure and keep the leg of lamb covered with a lid or plastic wrap.

Preheat oven to 350 degrees.

Remove lamb from refrigerator, sprinkle with salt and pepper. Bake uncovered for 2 ½ hours, depending on desired doneness. Baste with pan drippings frequently to keep the meat moist and juicy. Let rest for at least 15 minutes before carving. Serve with mint sauce (see page 65).

> Chef's notes – Don't forget your trusty meat thermometer. After roasting for about 1 ¾ hours, check the meat every 15 minutes so you don't over or under cook. The internal temperature should be 130 degrees for medium rare. Remember it is going to gain an additional 10 degrees when you let it rest prior to carving. This is also a great time to use your remote thermometer. Isn't technology cool.

Rack of Lamb
Serves 6

2 racks of ribs - 6 ribs each	*2 Tbs garlic, chopped*
¾ cups fine bread crumbs	*¼ cup fresh parsley, chopped*
Salt and pepper	*2 Tbs extra virgin olive oil*
1 tsp dried rosemary	*½ cup clarified butter*
¼ cup fresh mint, chopped	

Preheat oven to 500 degrees.

Toss the bread crumbs, salt and pepper, rosemary, mint, garlic, and parsley all together.

Trim most of the fat from the lamb and let it come to room temperature before cooking. Brush thoroughly with olive oil. Place rack of ribs, bone side up, in oiled roasting pan. Roast uncovered for about 10 minutes. Remove from oven. Reduce oven temperature to 400 degrees. Turn the lamb racks over. Cover with the bread crumb mixture. Spoon clarified butter gently over the crumbs. Put back into the oven and roast for 5 to 8 minutes more. The bread crumbs should be toasted to a golden brown. Don't forget your instant read thermometer and remember you will have some temperature increase while you are letting the lamb rest prior to carving. If the bread crumbs have browned nicely but the lamb is not done, cover with aluminum foil and place in a 300 degree oven until it is done.

You can carve this in the kitchen but I always find it makes for a very special dinner whenever you can carve at the table. Cut the ribs into single chops, two for each person. No sauce is required, but the reduced merlot sauce (see page 66) or the mint sauce (see page 65) is great with this dish.

> Chef's notes - This is an easy dish to make for company - it always gets ooohs and aaaahs when brought to the table. Everyone thinks it must be more complicated than it is.

Rabbit

Rabbit with Pesto and Mustard Sauce
Serves 5

2 - 3 pounds rabbit meat, de-boned	*½ cup heavy cream (you can substitute whole milk here, add 1 Tbs of butter)*
Pinch of salt	
Pinch of coarse ground pepper	*1 Tbs coarse grained mustard*
4 Tbs unsalted butter	*2 Tbs pesto (see page 65)*
½ cup dry white	

Cut the rabbit into bite sized pieces, season with salt and pepper. In a heavy skillet, over medium heat, melt 4 Tbs unsalted butter. Add the pieces of rabbit and sauté until the meat is cooked through; it will change to a whitish color. Remove from pan with slotted spoon and set aside.

Deglaze the pan with the wine and cook until the wine is reduced by half, stirring constantly with a wooden spoon making sure nothing sticks to the pan bottom. Add any juices that have collected on the plate where the rabbit has rested. Add the cream. Cook until the sauce begins to reduce and thicken a little bit. Remove from the heat and whisk the pesto and mustard into the sauce. Add the rabbit back into the pan with the sauce and cook just enough to reheat the rabbit.

Serve over egg noodles.

> Chef's notes – This recipe can also be made (and is delicious) with chicken, pork, or veal.

Apples with Caramel

Serves 6

1 cup sugar, divided	*2 Tbs lemon juice*
2 ½ Tbs water	*Pinch of allspice (or cinnamon)*
9 medium sized green apples (Granny Smiths or Pippins)	*5 eggs, whisked*
	¼ cup white rum or orange juice
1/3 cup butter	*1 cup sweetened whipped cream*

Remember caramel apples on a stick? This dish will bring back memories. Preheat oven to 350 degrees.

To make the caramel, put 2/3 cup of sugar and all the water into a sauce pan. Over high heat cook until the sugar melts and the mixture begins to turn golden brown. You have to stand there and stir and watch – it's cooking, it's cooking, it's burned. It happens that fast. So just stir and watch; it only takes a few minutes.

Once the sugar is browned, pour into a 2-quart oven proof glass bowl. Turn the melted caramel around the bowl coating the sides and bottom. Refrigerate until needed.

Peel and core the apples. Using the slicing blade on your food processor, slice the apples thinly, or you can use a mandolin. If you are so inclined, you can slice the apples with a paring knife. Melt the butter and pour into a baking pan. Add the sliced apples, add the lemon juice. Mix well so the apples are all coated with the butter and juice. Now mix the remaining 1/3 cup of sugar with the allspice (or cinnamon) and sprinkle the mixture over the apples making sure every piece is coated a little. Cook at 350 degrees for about 15 to 20 minutes, until apples are just tender-al dente.

In a large mixing bowl combine the eggs and rum, or orange juice. Fold in the cooked apples. Pour this mixture into the glass bowl on top of the caramelized sugar. Place in a water bath and bake in a 350 degree oven for about 50 to 60 minutes. Remove from the oven and let it rest for 10 minutes. Invert the bowl and release the apples and caramel on to a serving plate. Serve warm or cold with sweetened whipped cream.

Chef's notes – Be sure to use an oven proof <u>bowl</u> and not a rectangular casserole dish. The rounded sides of the bowl allow the caramel to release. If you use a casserole dish, the right angles in the corners won' let go of the caramel, and the dessert will be stuck in the dish.

Basque Cake

Serves 4-6

¼ cup toasted blanched almonds	1 egg
6 Tbs butter, well chilled	½ tsp almond extract
2 Tbs shortening, well chilled	3 Tbs ice water
1 ½ cups flour	Jar of plum jam
Pinch of salt	Powdered sugar for dusting
¼ cup sugar	

Preheat oven to 400 degrees.

Place the almonds in the food processor with the "S" blade. Pulse until finely ground. Add the butter, shortening, flour, salt, sugar, and wiz another minute, or until everything is mixed well. Leave ingredients in the processor bowl.

In another small bowl, separate the egg. Take the egg yolk and whisk together with the almond extract and chilled water. Turn the food processor onto a medium speed and pour egg mixture through the opening in the top. Process until the mixture begins to form a ball. Remove from the food processor, form into a ball. Place in mixing bowl, cover with plastic wrap and refrigerate for about 1 hour.

Roll about 2/3 of the dough into a circular shape onto a floured surface. Using a plate or a small cake pan as a pattern, cut out a piece of dough. Remove the unwanted trim and fold the round pastry in half and transfer to an un-greased baking sheet and unfold it. Evenly spread about ¾ cup of plum jam onto the dough leaving about ½" naked all around the edge. Roll out the remaining third of the dough, this layer will be thinner than the first. Whisk up the egg white, brush around the ½ inch naked part. With the remaining dough, cut the same sized circle and place on top the jam, lining up with the bottom layer. Gently press the edges with your fingers or with the tines of a fork. With a very sharp paring knife, cut and remove sections from the top layer of dough to create a wheel spoke pattern, exposing the jam layer. Bake in a 400 degree oven for about 15 minutes, or until lightly browned. Remove from the oven and sprinkle with powdered sugar. Serve hot or cold.

Basque Rice Pudding
Serves 6

1 quart whole milk	Pinch of ground cinnamon
4 cinnamon sticks	A tiny pinch of allspice and freshly grated nutmeg
3 cups washed long grain white rice	
2 eggs, whisked	1 Tbs honey
1 ½ tsp cornstarch	½ cup sugar

Heat ½ the milk and the cinnamon sticks in a medium sauce pan, do not boil. Add the rice, cover and simmer for approximately 30 minutes. Remove cinnamon sticks.

Whisk the eggs into the remaining cold milk. Add most of the cornstarch, whisk some more. You can always add a bit more corn starch if needed, but you don't want to over thicken the pudding.

Mix the rice mixture into the cold egg mixture, one tablespoon at a time, until the egg mixture is heated through and through. You need to add egg mixture to rice mixture slowly so you don't cook the egg. Add allspice and nutmeg, the sugar and honey. When it is all combined, place back on the stove and bring to a boil. If the pudding still needs more thickening you can add a little more cornstarch dissolved in water. Make sure to constantly stir the pudding

Can be served hot or chilled, with a dash of cinnamon on top. Sometimes I add raisins or pistachios when it's cooking, just because it's good. The perfect ending to a perfect meal. An easy to make, easy to eat, yummy simple dessert. Who doesn't like rice pudding?

Chocolate Bread Pudding
Serves 10

1 lb stale bread (approximately 1 loaf)	½ tsp vanilla
3 eggs, whisked	Pinch of salt
1 cup sugar	Cinnamon and sugar sprinkle
2 ½ cups milk	Whipped cream
1 ¼ cup chocolate sauce	

Mix eggs, sugar, milk, chocolate sauce, vanilla, and salt together. Cut bread into cubes (or process in the food processor to very coarsely ground bread crumbs). Place wet ingredients and bread crumbs into a large bowl, making sure all the bread is submerged below the surface of the chocolate mixture. Pour into buttered 9x12 baking dish. Cover and refrigerate for one hour.

Preheat oven to 350 degrees. Remove cover from pudding and place into a water bath and bake for 45 minutes. A knife inserted into center will come out clean when it's done. Remove from oven and sprinkle with cinnamon and sugar. Serve hot with additional chocolate sauce and whipped cream.

Chef's notes – This dessert serves a lot of people easily and is always a hit. It can be reheated in the oven as long as you use a water bath and cover it.

A woman who works at our restaurant loves this dessert. She makes it at home and scoops out single serving portions onto a cookie sheet and freezes it. Once they are frozen solid, she puts them into a zip lock freezer bag and always has dessert on hand. She removes them, one at a time, and microwaves it for a couple minutes, and bida boom bida bang, she has a great dessert ready to serve.

Coconut Macaroons

Makes 36 macaroons

1 can sweetened condensed milk	1 tsp vanilla
2 10-oz bags of shredded sweetened coconut	2 whisked eggs
	1 pinch of salt

Preheat oven to 325 degrees.
Add all ingredients to a mixing bowl and fold gently until well blended.
Spoon golf ball sized cookies onto a cookie sheet lined with parchment paper. Do not roll cookies into balls; you want them somewhat loose with the coconut pieces sticky outty all over the place. Cook for approximately 15 minutes or until cookies are golden on the bottom and the coconut on the top is browned.

Chef's notes – This recipe makes about 3 dozen cookies. You will need to make more. After the macaroons have cooled you can melt chocolate chips and individually dip the cookies into the melted chocolate to make chocolate macaroons. Instead of vanilla, try substituting lemon, rum, or almond extract to make different flavors. If you decide to do lemon ones, add some zest as well.

Crème Brulee

Serves 6

2 ½ cups whole milk	4 egg yolks
½ cup heavy cream	½ cup sugar

Combine the milk and cream in a sauce pan. Heat to just boiling and then remove from heat.

In a separate bowl, beat the egg yolks vigorously. Add the sugar while beating the mixture. Now here comes the tricky part: If you add the hot cream too quickly to the egg yolks, you will cook the eggs. Instead, slowly whisk the hot cream into the eggs (about ¼ cup at a time), continuously stirring the mixture. Return mixture to sauce pan and place on very low heat. Slowly stir the mixture so it doesn't clump. Remove from heat and pour the mixture into small ovenproof ramekins and chill in the refrigerator for at least 3 hours. Now comes the fun part: Sprinkle a very thin layer of sugar on the top of each of the ramekins and get out your trusty blow torch and toast the top of the sugar until it becomes brown and a crust forms. Serve immediately to ooooohhhs and ahhhhhhhs.

Decadent Chocolate Mousse
Serves 6

24 ounces semi sweet chocolate chips	½ cup powdered sugar
3 Tbs instant coffee	8 egg whites
½ cup almond liquor	Pinch of salt
4 egg yolks	½ cup almond paste (see page 58)
1 cup whipping cream	Crème fraische (see page 63)

Chocolate, chocolate, chocolate. It doesn't get any better than this!

Melt chocolate in the microwave about 2 minutes. Stir and make sure it is thoroughly melted. If not, microwave it another minute. Watch it. Stir it again. It burns quickly. Don't over microwave it. When completely melted, add instant coffee and almond liquor. Allow the chocolate to cool, but do not allow it to re-harden.

In a separate bowl, whisk egg yolks and slowly add to the chocolate mixture. In another bowl, whip the cream and add sugar slowly, beat until stiff. Fold into chocolate and egg mixture. In another bowl, whip egg whites with a pinch of salt.

Slowly fold the whipped egg whites, in batches, into the whipped cream and chocolate/egg mixture. Be careful not to over mix the mousse, or you will lose all of the air you've captured in the whipping process.

Gently fold in the almond paste. Dish up into individual dessert dishes. Chill in the refrigerator for at least 3 hours. Serve with crème fraische.

Fancy Chocolate Almond Crème
Serves 12

1 cup water	*½ cup toasted blanched almonds, coarsely ground*
1/3 cup sugar	*2 cups whipping cream*
4 oz chocolate chips	*2 dozen ladyfingers*
½ lb butter	*Shaved chocolate*
3 Tbs dark rum	*Sweetened whipped cream*
¼ tsp almond extract	

Combine sugar and water in a glass measuring cup. Microwave until sugar is completely dissolved. You now have a "simple syrup."

Melt chocolate chips in the microwave until melted. Every microwave is different, so cook on high for 2 minutes, remove and stir to make sure it's melted. You may need to add more time to melt completely, but be careful not to burn it. You have to take it out of the microwave and give it a stir at the 2 minute mark. Sometimes the chocolate chips retain their shape even though they are melted – don't ask me why – it's a mystery how they do that, but stir them up and check to make sure they are melted. Allow the chocolate to cool, but do not allow it to re-harden.

Using the "S" steel blade in the food processor, begin to process the melted chocolate with the simple syrup. Add butter, 2 Tbs at a time, and then add rum, almond extract, and ground almonds. Remove from food processor and set aside in a large mixing bowl in the refrigerator to cool. Whip 2 cups of unsweetened whipping cream until stiff, fold into chilled chocolate mixture.

Split the lady fingers. Use enough split lady fingers to line the bottom and sides of a spring form pan. Set the remaining split lady fingers aside on a cookie sheet. Make another batch of simple syrup and place in a spray bottle. Spray the split lady fingers lining the spring form pan. Then spray the remaining split lady fingers on the cookie sheet.

Spoon 1/3 of the chocolate mixture into the spring form pan on top of the lady fingers. Arrange another layer of lady fingers on top of the chocolate, trimming them so they fit closely and completely. Add two more layers of the chocolate mixture and lady fingers. You should have 3 layers of chocolate.

When the final layer of lady fingers is on the top, weigh it down with a plate to firmly compact all the layers. Refrigerate overnight (or at least 6 hours). The butter and chocolate must be chilled firmly so the dessert will hold its shape.

When ready to serve, place on a flat serving dish. Remove the plate from the top of the dessert and remove the sides of the spring form pan. Decorate and serve with whipped cream and shaved chocolate.

Flan
Serves 6

Caramel

1 cup sugar	¼ cup water

Pour sugar and water into a sauce pan and cook over medium heat until the sugar melts and turns to the color of dark rum. Caramel burns fast. Watch and stir it constantly, don't blink, don't go talk on the phone. It only takes about 5 minutes. It is cooking, it is cooking, and it is burnt! That fast. So watch it. When it reaches the color of dark rum, pour immediately into individual ramekins. It will harden as it cools.

Milk Mixture

1 qt whole milk	2 sticks whole cinnamon

Gently boil milk and cinnamon in a heavy sauce pan for about 10 minutes. Do not cover, set aside to cool.

Egg Mixture

5 eggs	½ cup sugar

Preheat oven to 350 degrees.

Whisk eggs until they are light and frothy. Add sugar and whisk until well blended. After the milk has cooled, strain it, removing the cinnamon stick and any milk scum that may have formed. Add strained and cooled milk mixture to the egg mixture and mix well. Be sure milk is cooled before adding to the eggs, or it will cook the eggs. Pour egg and milk mixture into the individual ramekins with the caramel. Place filled ramekins into a shallow pan of water (water bath) where the water comes about half way up each ramekin. Cook in the oven at 350 degrees. Because every oven is different, check for doneness at 20 minutes. Insert a toothpick occasionally to check. When the toothpick comes out clean the custard is done.

Once cooked, place ramekins in refrigerator and cool for about 3 hours. To serve, take a straight table knife and run around the edges of each ramekin. Place a dessert plate over each ramekin and invert. Serve immediately.

If you are new to wine, or you have been at it for a while, there is always something else to know and learn. I know winemakers who have huge, glamorous, and expensive wineries and tasting rooms. I also know little guys who have a tasting room in their processing facility, with a tasting bar made out of two barrels and a wooden barn plank. They both can make exceptional wines. If you are new to the experience, think of wine tasting as an adult treasure hunt. It is an incredibly fun experience to discover something you think is wonderful to drink and then get to share with your friends. Telling them how you found it often makes for great dinner conversation.

Be advised the price is not always an indicator as to whether it is good or not. I've tasted some very expensive wines that I personally think are just ok, and I've tasted some that are not expensive at all and they can knock my socks off.

People ask me all the time, "how do you know if wine is good or not?" The honest to goodness answer is this: *If you like it, it's good. If you don't, it's not*. It is that simple. If you are new at this, don't expect to try a very expensive, big, bold red wine and think it is wonderful. Do you remember when you had your first beer? You probably didn't think it tasted that great. You develop a taste for it and it sort of grows on you. Think of wine in the same way, only it can cost quite a bit more than beer.

If you are just starting to develop your wine palate, start by drinking the lighter wines. Rose's are delicate and light. Pinot Noir's are lighter bodied than their darker bolder cousins. Try white wines; discover the difference between chardonnays that are made in oak barrels and chardonnays that are made in stainless steel tanks. You would think the ones from the expensive oak barrels must be better, but my wife only likes the kind made in stainless steel tanks. Everyone's taster is different. That is also why it is such a satisfying and fun experience.

You will see the term "estate wines" on labels. That means the grapes are grown on the winery's land and managed by the winemaker from berry to bottle. Most of the real big guys grow all their own grapes, but they also source blending wines from other growers. There are growers who don't make any wine at all. They sell all their fruit to winemakers. Sometimes the fruit can be shipped hundreds of miles to a winery several counties over. I've even heard of grapes that are shipped across state lines to be processed into wine. Sometimes just the juice from grapes is shipped. You don't have to be a huge, several hundred acre vineyard to be in the wine business. You can have 2 to 5 acres and still make some money if you are growing a particularly splendid wine grape.

Some folks have "hobby" vineyards and only make wine for their friends and family. But, trust me; don't get caught up in the glamour of the vineyard lifestyle

and beautiful surroundings. It is still farming and not for the faint of heart. It's a difficult business with all the pitfalls and trials of any other agricultural business. Sometimes there is a glut of grapes (over production); bugs and other pests can destroy your entire year's work; it can rain just before harvest and mildew your entire vineyard; your neighbors can drive you crazy because they don't farm and the zon guns (propane cannons used to frighten away the birds as fruit ripens) can make you want to kill each other. But there is a beautiful rhythm to the whole process as well.

Spring and fall both bring their own challenges and lists of things to be done. Summertime is always busy in the vineyard just keeping up with weeding and thinning and canopy control. Harvest time can be magical. It also means long days of hard labor picking fruit and getting it into the winery at the proper brix (brix – amount of sugar in the fruit) It is a massive amount of effort and the wine making process every year is different from the last as far as what you end up with. Good wines start in the vineyard. You cannot make spectacular wines from less than spectacular fruit.

Wine Tasting

The best way to learn about wines it to taste a lot of them. Discover what you like. Visit tasting rooms. Tasting room etiquette is something no one ever tells you about. You sort of learn it by trial and error; sometimes a dirty look is most educational.

Let me give you some information here that may save you some awkward moments. Forget everything your mother taught you about spitting. It is perfectly acceptable; in fact the majority of wineries encourage you to use the spit bucket. Why? They want you to enjoy wine while you are vertical, not horizontal. For every ounce of wine you take in, try to take in an equal amount of water as you go through your tasting tour for the day. It helps a lot. Eat something. Bring food with you if you are going into an area where there are no restaurants. Most wineries have lovely spots to picnic, so bring one with you. Enjoy the day. Relax, smell the roses. Don't try to do too many wineries in one day. Five or six seem to be the magic number. More than that, your taster quits working.

If you smoke, try to hold off until you get back to where you are staying. Most smokers don't realize how long the odor of smoke clings to their clothing. Wine tasting involves smelling before drinking and cigarette smoke can be very distracting. The same can be said for heavy perfumes and colognes. Ladies, do not wear thick lipsticks or glosses. They usually have their own fragrance and taste, not to mention it is most difficult to remove from glassware.

Bring a cooler and keep your picnic lunch in there. When you are finished, store your wine in the cooler. The temperature in a closed car can reach wine killing degrees in a very short time. By keeping your wine in the cooler you can help save it from the damaging heat.

Turn your cell phone off. Treat the tasting room staff with courtesy and re-spect. I encourage you to ask them questions. Take notes. Don't over indulge. Generally speaking, the tasting room staff will go out of their way to make sure you have a good experience while you are at their tasting room. If you are a newbie,

tell them, they will help you. If you are an old hat, they love that too. For the most part, they are knowledgeable and a valuable source of information about what is going on in their appellation, from where to eat dinner to what festival is coming up. Sometimes the wine tasting person is also the wine making person. It is always a fun and pleasurable day when you interact with the tasting room staff.

You may choose to hire someone else to drive, or bring someone who agrees to be the designated driver. There are usually wine tour services available who will take you on a very nice wine tasting tour with other people in a small van or bus. Limo's are available who specialize in tasting tours. I've even seen people do it on bicycles.

Dress comfortably. Wine cannot tell if you are in shorts or a tux. Wear shoes that allow you to easily walk on cement or gravel; you will be traipsing across lots of different ground and surfaces as you hunt for wine treasure.

Let me share with you how I taste wine. I've tasted lots of wine and I have learned these techniques from people who have been at it a lot longer than I have.

1. Hold your glass up to the light and examine the color and clarity.

2. Swirl the wine around the glass and stick your entire nose into the glass and take a deep whiff.

3. Take a small sip and let it run under your tongue. Suck in some air through your lips with the wine still in your mouth; you are trying to aerate the wine. (Note - if you sound like Uncle Fred slurping soup that is too hot, you are doing it right.)

4. Move the wine to the back of your throat and swallow, or spit. Pay attention to the flavors that come to your mind as you go through this process.

Wine flavors are referred to as "notes" (like musical notes). Make written observations as you go so you can differentiate what you tasted and liked. If you don't take notes, it can all run together by the end of the day. Always try to buy at least one bottle of wine from each tasting room. It's not just a free wine tour. If you fall in love with something, buy a case; if it is a small operation, next time you come by it's quite possible they won't have any more.

Have fun and enjoy the process.

* * *

Wine has its own jargon like any other specialty. Here are a few words and definitions so you at least sound like you know what you are doing. Taste is a very broad term; there are several ways to talk about the way something tastes.

Touch or Feel - the sensations your mouth experiences, whether something is full bodied and round or weak and unbalanced.

Tannins - Always more present in red wines than whites, they come from the stems and skins and seeds. Red wines are exposed longer to these things. Soft tannins will leave a dry, not sweet, sensation in your mouth. When tannins are high, they are called harsh tannins. Harsh tannins leave an astringent feeling in the back of your throat, sometimes referred to as "bite."

Sugar - The amount of alcohol created in wine is produced by the amount of sugar concentrated in the grape harvest. The term "residual sugar" is tossed around a lot. It means how much sugar you can actually taste in the wine and how much sugar is still present after bottling.

- Dry - no sensation of any sugar

- Slightly sweet - the first hint of any sweetness

- Medium sweet - more sweetness than just a hint

- Sweet - no mistaking that there is a lot of sugar left in the wine

- Very sweet - almost a sugary syrupy sweetness

- Cloying - An over powering sensation of sweetness, too sweet

Alcohol - If there is too much alcohol content in a bottle of wine, it causes a burning sensation in your mouth. If there is not enough, the wine will seem watery or wimpy. When properly balanced, it produces body and richness. Too much alcohol is not a good thing in wines. Some wines are intentionally fortified with additional alcohol; ports and Sherries are fortified.

Acid – Acid is an important element in wines that helps determine its flavor. The ideal is to have a balance between acids and the other properties in wine. Too much acid and it will taste sour or tart, too little and it will be flat or flabby.

Balance - You will hear this term used all the time. It is not about how well you walk after you have been wine tasting all day. It means that the tannins, sugar, alcohol, and acids all work together. It is how well the winemaker is able to create this balance that makes for a great bottle of wine. Robert Lewis Stevenson once said "Wine is poetry in a bottle". Think of the winemaker as the poet.

Flavor - Before your tongue ever tastes it, your nose will tell you what to expect from a wine. 85% of what you smell accounts for what you think of as flavor. The term "nose" is used all the time to describe what wine smells like.

Finish - After you have swallowed or spit your wine sample, the final assessment of what your mouth feels and tastes is called "the finish".

Fruit Forward - Meaning the notes of fruit are apparent before you notice other characteristics of the wine. Even though wines are usually made from grapes, they amazingly can have notes of many different things like plums, jam, currents, strawberries, and even tropical fruits like guava and pineapple. Close your eyes and let your tongue tell you what you taste. Sometimes the flavor of fruit is not what you taste first; in that case, it is not a fruit forward style.

Pairing Wines with Food

Back in the day it was easy to pair wine. White wine for fish and chicken; red wine with hearty meats and spaghetti. Today, due to the influence of ethnic foods and the expanding variety of wine varietals available, the rules are much looser and it takes a little better palate to do well.

Here are a few rules of thumb to keep in mind when you are menu planning. Let me remind you of my most stead fast rule – "if you like it, it's good." There are many varietals and blends available, too many to go into here. I'm just going to touch on a few to get you started.

Aperitifs - Sherry, sparkling wines, and many white table wines. Served before or between meals. Usually served well chilled without food. Can be served with nuts, cheeses, and appetizers as the beginning of a great feast, or by themselves as a light afternoon respite. They are designed to get your palate working.

White Wines - Sauvignon Blanc, Chardonnay, Pinot Blanc, Viognier, Rieslings, Fume Blanc. Usually served with lighter spicier dishes. Normally served chilled and paired with chicken, fish, shell fish, pork, omelets, and many Asian dishes. Whenever whites are blended they are referred to as a "table wine."

Red Wines - Barbera, Merlot, Nebbiolo, Petit Syrah, Syrah or Shiraz (they are the same grape), Zinfandel, Cabernet Sauvignon, are all varietals. Many are blends like Bordeaux from France. Meritage is another term used for blends. Blends are fast becoming the new trend in red wines as winemakers try to create something that is more interesting or better balanced than a single variety. I have tasted some spectacular blends, and I have had some that need to go back to the drawing board. When blended with other varietals, red wines are also referred to as a "table wine". These big bold reds are best served with hearty dishes. Usually served at room temperature. Pair with steaks, chops, roasts, pastas with red sauce, and even hamburgers. Hearty dishes need a hearty wine. White wine nuances usually get lost when up against a savory pot roast. But if that is what you like to drink with pot roast - don't let the "rules" get in the way, drink what you enjoy.

Dessert Wines - Muscats, Late Harvest, Port, ahhhhhh. Any of these are at their best when served with any kind of chocolate. They are also perfectly paired with fruit tarts, crème brulee, cheese cake, cake, cupcakes, cookies, and macaroons.

Sparkling Wines - Only sparkling wines from the Champagne region of France can be truly called champagne. Some people get real testy about it. Champagne has become a generic name for all sparkling wines, even though they are not true champagne. The not so secret, secret is that California is producing world-class sparkling wines that rival anything from France. Sparkling wines and champagne are classified by the amount of residual sugar from natural (very dry), brut (dry) extra dry (semi-dry) sec (sweet) and demi-sec (also sweet) styles. You can serve a sparkling wine with anything. Serve it chilled with appetizers, main courses, as well as desserts. It's about celebration; celebrate every chance you get. Life is short. Drink the good wine!

Cuvees, Meritages, & Hermitages – A very fancy name for blended wines – aka "table wine." Some of best and most expensive wines in the world can be a blend.

Born and raised in Southern California, Chef Dallas has had an eclectic life to put it lightly. From sailing the South Pacific in his sailboat, developing real estate, to growing grapes, making wine and creating extraordinary meals from his famous little café.

For the past twenty years he has been intimately involved in the wine and food genre leading up to his present position as executive chef and owner of the Tenth Street Basque Café. For years his guests have clamored for his tightly guarded recipes which he has finally agreed to share.

Chef Dallas currently lives on his ranch with his family on the Central Coast of California.